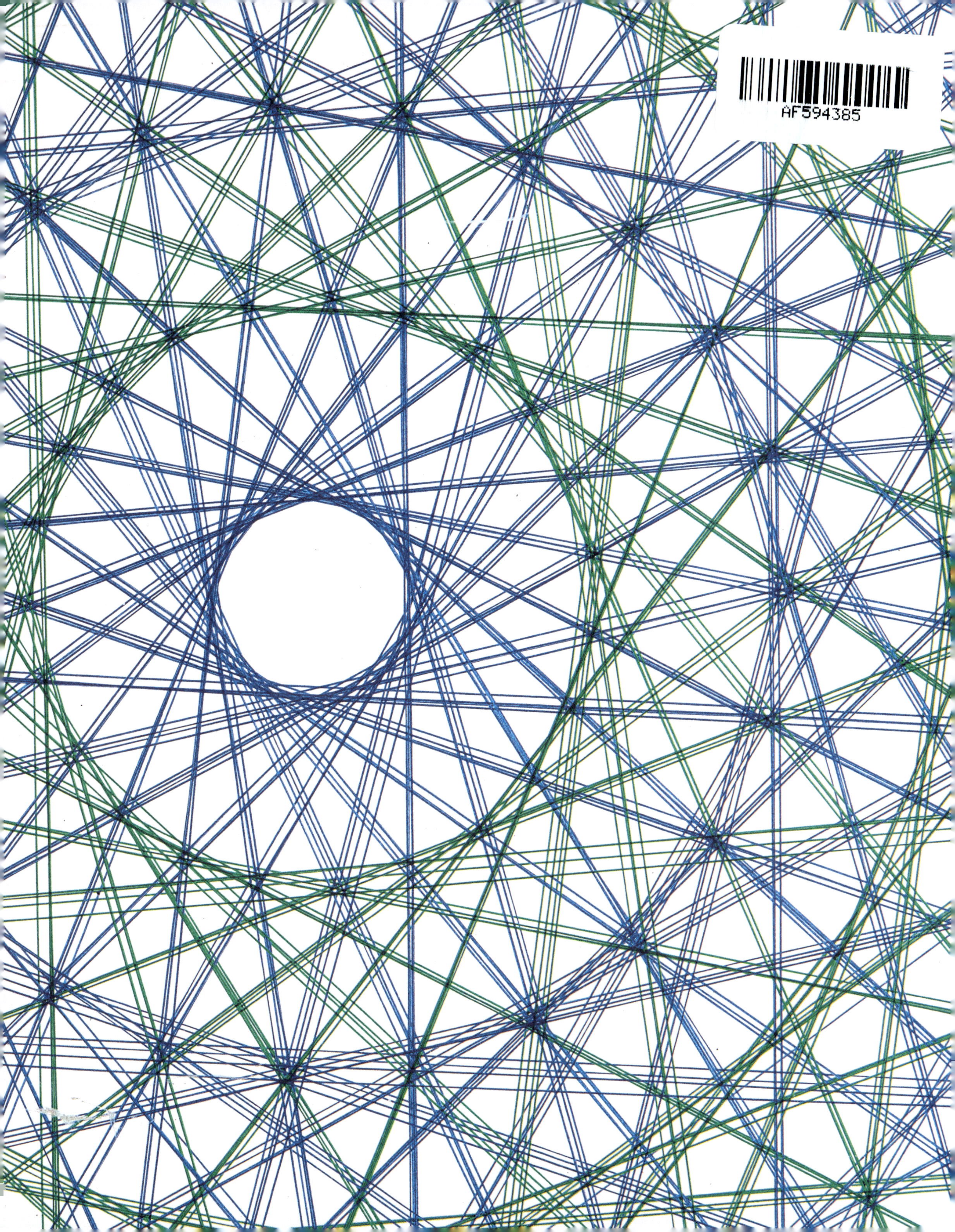

SUE FULLER

Into the Composition

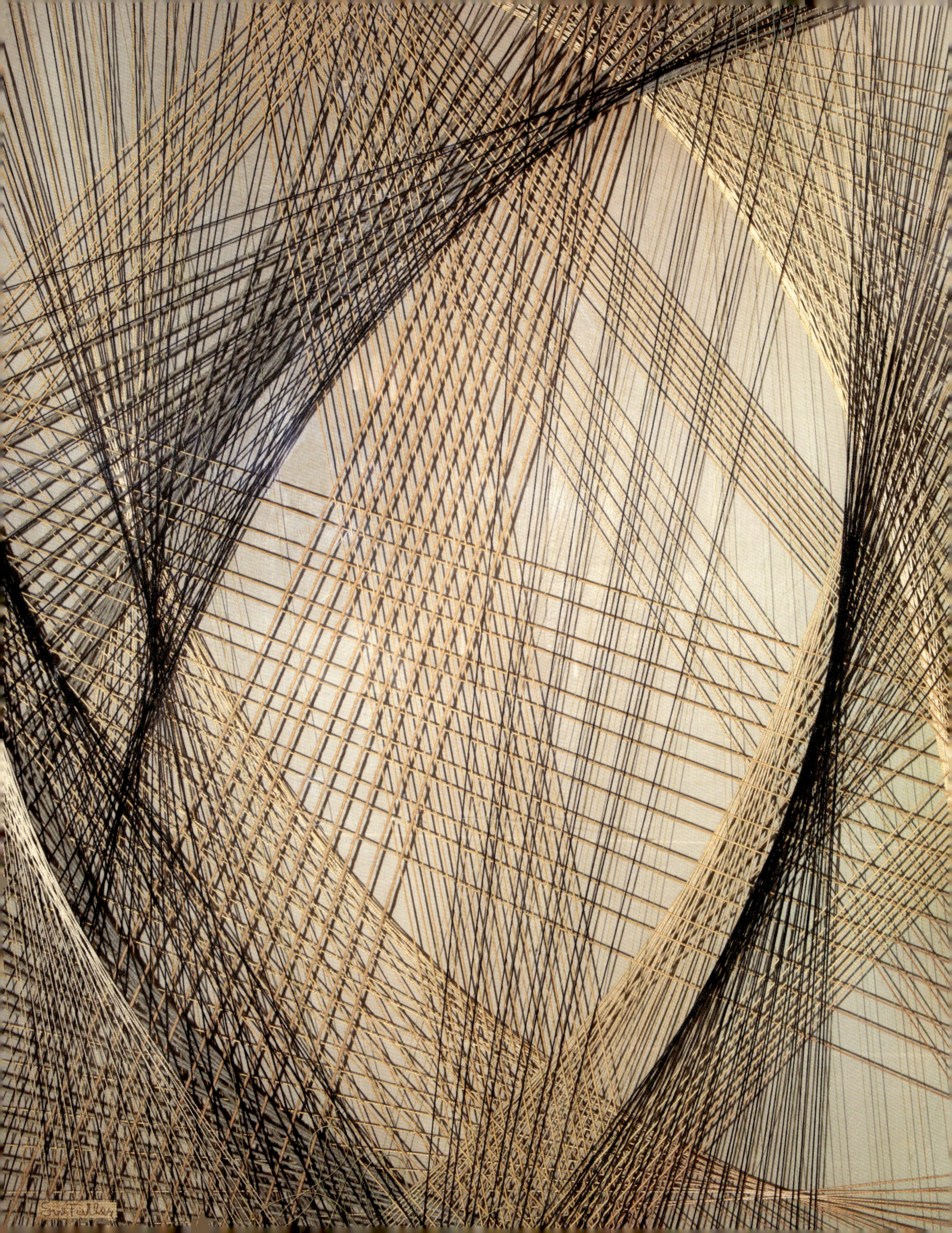

SUE FULLER

INTO THE COMPOSITION

Texts by Alex J. Taylor and Christina Weyl

LUXEMBOURG + CO.

Ridinghouse

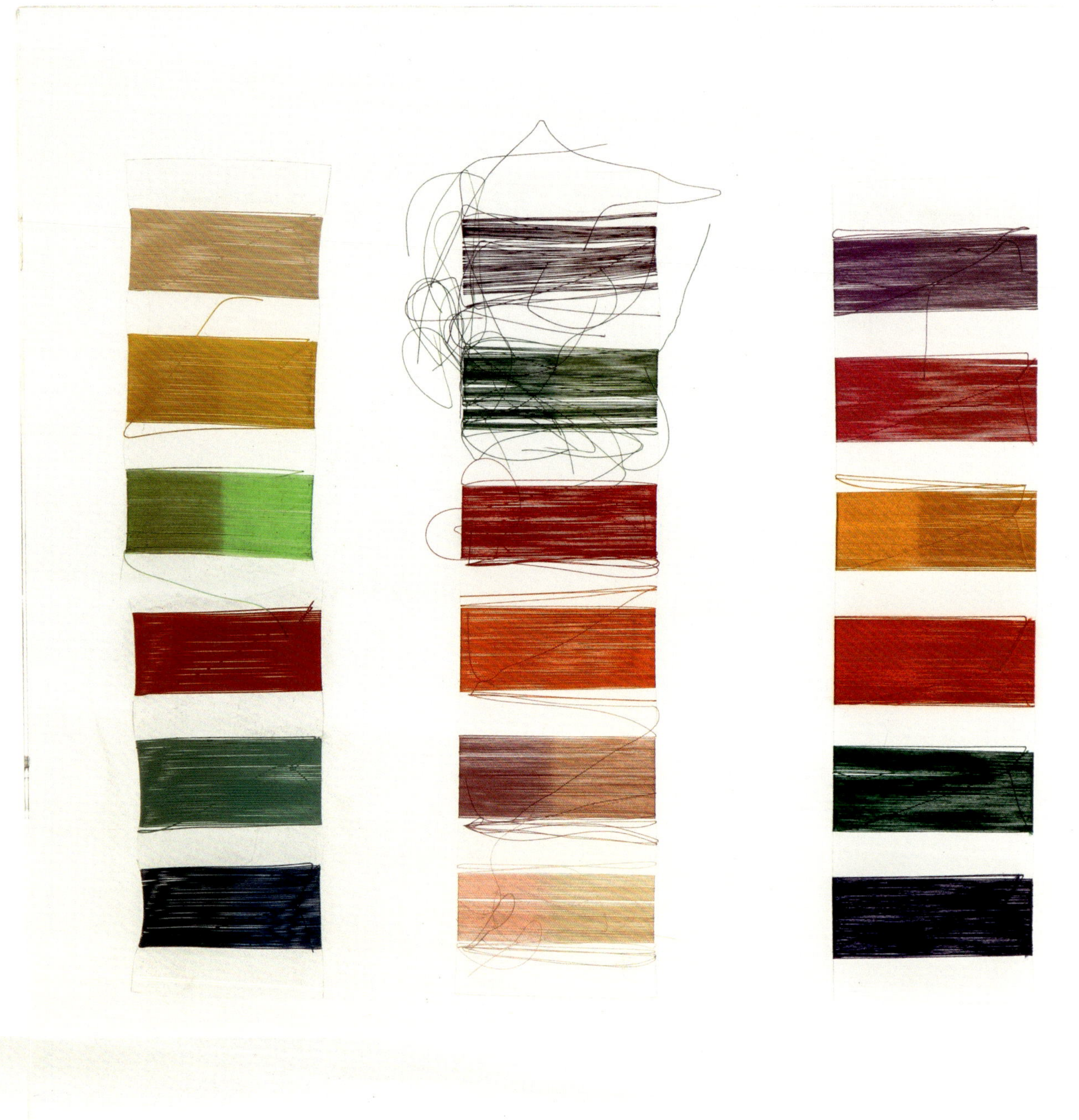

Contents

Sue Fuller:
Into the Composition

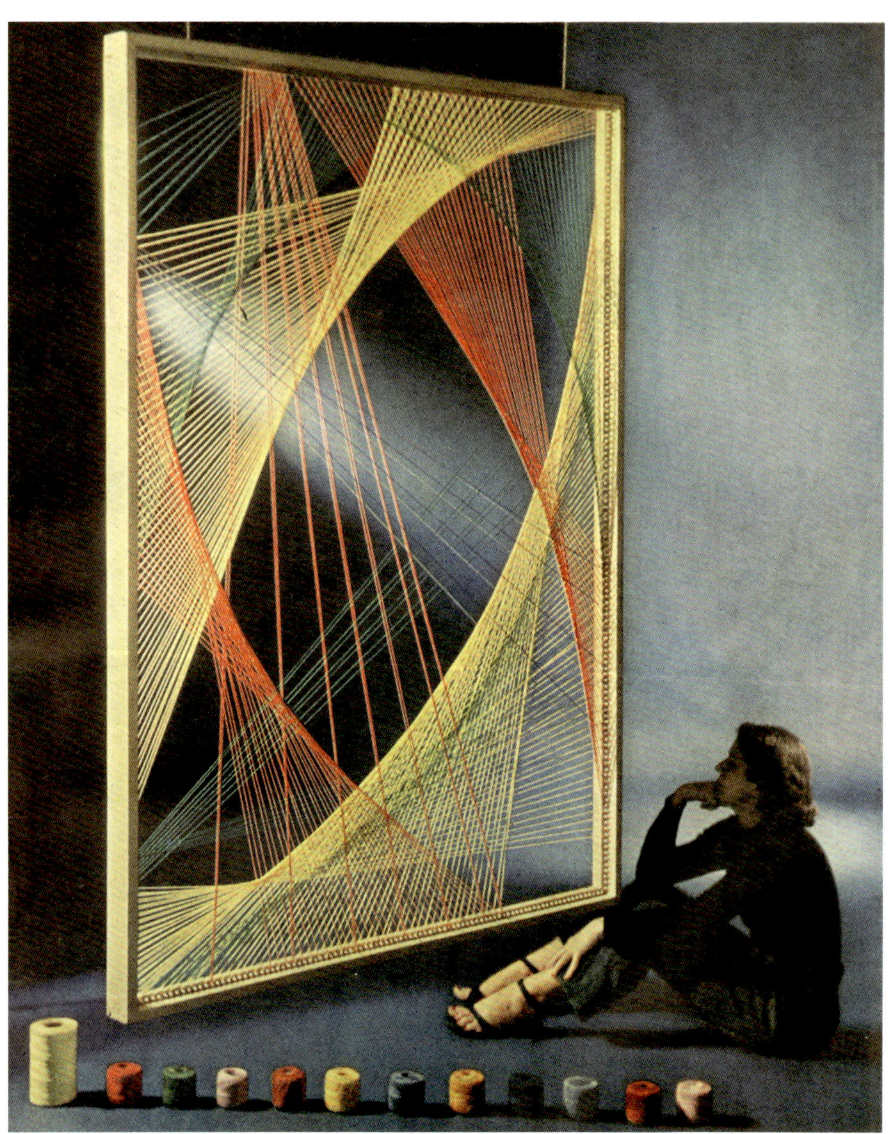

Fig.1
Photograph of Sue Fuller with a string composition, from a feature in *Life*, 31 October 1949

Imagine an entire universe that hangs by a thread. A complex structure of colours and shapes, balancing forces and weight, all held in absolute precision by a few fishing lines: taut, strong, colourful but nevertheless precarious by nature, as if floating in mid-air. Sue Fuller (1914–2006) began making three-dimensional string compositions in 1946, at a time when North American art was largely invested in principles of improvisation and intuitive abstract expression. Opposing the trend of her time, she chose to work with restraint and accuracy, calculating the structural skeleton of each of her works with great rigour, thereby drawing more on the influence of the Bauhaus school and its émigré teachers and students, who brought their ideas and work to the United States in the 1930s, than the spirit of the local, more dominant New York School that was active in the 1950s and 1960s.

An independent thinker and a gifted maker, Fuller was invested in the links between form and function, pattern and creative outcome, and she embraced interdisciplinarity. In her hands, these ideas came to gain a new interpretation, developed from, but different to, the principles of the Bauhaus and other pre-war tendencies that called for the union of technology, design and art. The daughter of a construction engineer, she followed a highly competitive academic path at Carnegie Institute of Technology, Columbia University and Stanley William Hayter's Atelier 17, located at the New School for Social Research.[1] Fuller's progression as an artist was underlined by a parallel trajectory as a researcher and teacher, which she pursued across several institutions with the support of intellectual bodies such as the Guggenheim Foundation and the National Institute of Arts and Letters.

After some years working in the media of drawing, painting and printmaking, her experimentation with production methods – predominantly the use of lace and thread as materials that lend themselves easily to the formation of grid-like compositions and rhythmic lines – led Fuller to create her first group of string compositions, executed sometime in 1947–48. From this point onwards, her meticulous geometric constructions in string came to represent at once the delicate precision of a seamstress and the force and stability of an industrial manufacturer. Small systems and networks of string, Fuller's *String Compositions*, as they became known, were made according to predetermined rhythmic patterns, only occasionally undermined by loosely arranged or irregular shapes – a string meandering atop the composition, or an uneven distribution of spaces between certain diagonal lines. Yet no details in Fuller's compositions ever occurred incidentally, nor did she leave the resulting artefact vulnerable to the risks of erosion, fading or unravelling. Fuller invested efforts in anticipating what conservation of her work might look like, which led her to encase each of her creations in boxes or between plates of acrylic glass, conserving colour and tension to the utmost degree possible, as their current condition confirms. From the 1950s her work became the subject of much institutional interest, having

Fig.2
Anni Albers (1899–1994)
Knot, 1947
Gouache on paper
12¼ × 9¾ in. (31.1 × 24.7 cm)
The Josef and Anni Albers Foundation, Bethany, CT

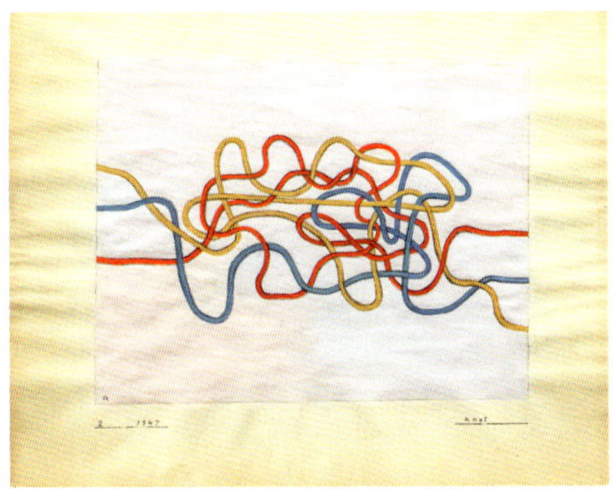

1 Hayter's Atelier 17 was a studio, school and hub for artists working in printmaking. It opened its doors in Paris in 1927 and moved to New York in 1940.

been included in the celebrated exhibitions *Abstract Painting and Sculpture in America* (1951, fig.5) and *The Responsive Eye* (1963), both at the Museum of Modern Art, New York. In the wave of acquisitions that followed, Fuller's work made its way to the Philadelphia Museum of Art, the Whitney Museum of American Art, the Art Institute of Chicago, the Museum of Modern Art and the Tate in London, among other collections.

But Fuller's position, historically speaking, was once more challenged by the politics of art in relation to other tendencies. Artists associated with Pop and Conceptual art, but also with second-wave feminism, deemed her practice too closely invested in traditions of craft – particularly as a woman practitioner – and too far removed from conceptual critique of consumerist culture or gender politics. The truth, however, was far from it. Fuller had direct engagement with technological development, methods of production and material culture, and her work was raising questions about the alienation of fine art as a discipline from other traditions of creative activity.

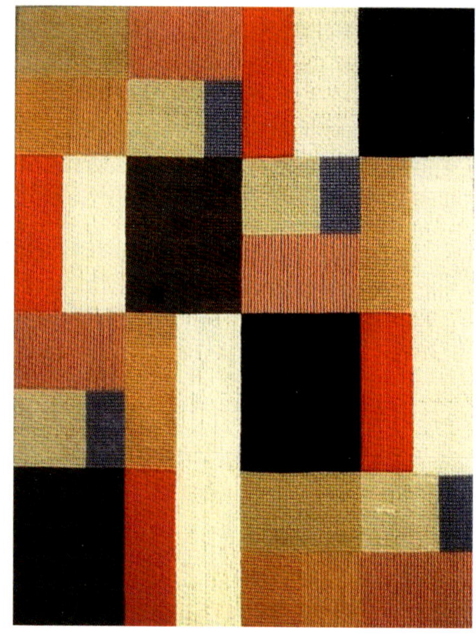

Fig.3
Sophie Taeuber-Arp (1889–1943)
Vertical-Horizontal Composition, 1916
Wool on canvas
19¾ × 15⅛ in. (50 × 38.5 cm)
Fondazione Marguerite Arp, Locarno

The exhibition *Sue Fuller: Into the Composition* and this accompanying publication form the first major monographic study of Fuller's work since her death in 2006. Her ambitious and experimental practice is perhaps unique in its characteristics, but it also partakes in a long line of inspiring practitioners whose interest in the connection between art and craft informed their work and presented an opposition to prevailing tendencies in their times. This includes artists such as Anni Albers (fig.2), Sophie Taeuber-Arp (fig.3), Lygia Clark (fig.4) and Irma Blank, to name but a few. Like them, Fuller's absence from the canon of abstract art in the second half of the twentieth century is at odds with her contribution to both stylistic as well as technological developments in the arts during this period. Her openness to the lessons of design, craft and technological innovation in the service of art did not always coincide with mainstream trends in North American art during her lifetime. But for Fuller, other inquiries were more important. Determined to achieve 'Balance, motion, suspension' and 'tension' in her work, as she noted in her application for a Guggenheim Fellowship in 1948, Fuller went as far as identifying new materials and production methods by collaborating with industrial manufacturers to produce the polypropylene 'fishing line' monofilament that she thought best suited for her practice, obtaining a US patent on the way for the process by which she constructed her work.

Fig.4
Lygia Clark (1920–1988)
Bicho, 1962
Aluminium
7⅞ × 7⅞ × 9⅞ in. (20 × 20 × 25 cm)

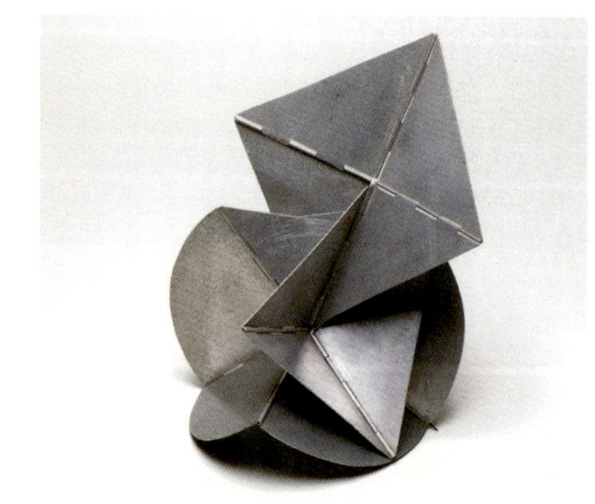

Fuller believed that art-making is a rigorous practice that must reflect advances in both science and the humanities, and her work, as a result, defies conventions of artistic medium. 'It's very difficult for people to decide whether I'm a painter or a sculptor,' she once explained, 'I really don't know myself.' To these two titles one should add engineer, innovator and teacher. Like time capsules carried across more than half a century, her unique and remarkable artworks now raise the question: What if? What if Abstract Expressionism allowed for an alternative approach to emerge alongside it? What if second-wave feminism had acknowledged abstraction as a force? What if we look at Fuller's work again today: what will we find?

We wish to thank Susan Teller, Fuller's long-time gallerist and friend, for her advice along the way, as well as the Sue Fuller Estate, Berta Walker, Janet Ruttenberg and Eric Ruttenberg for their support of the project. We also thank Michael Battalia for bringing to light new archival materials, as well as Alex J. Taylor and Christina Weyl for their illuminating scholarly contributions to this book and original perspectives on Fuller's life and work. Finally, we thank the various lenders who made this project possible.

Luxembourg + Co.

Fig.5
Installation view of *Abstract Painting and Sculpture in America*, The Museum of Modern Art, New York, 1951

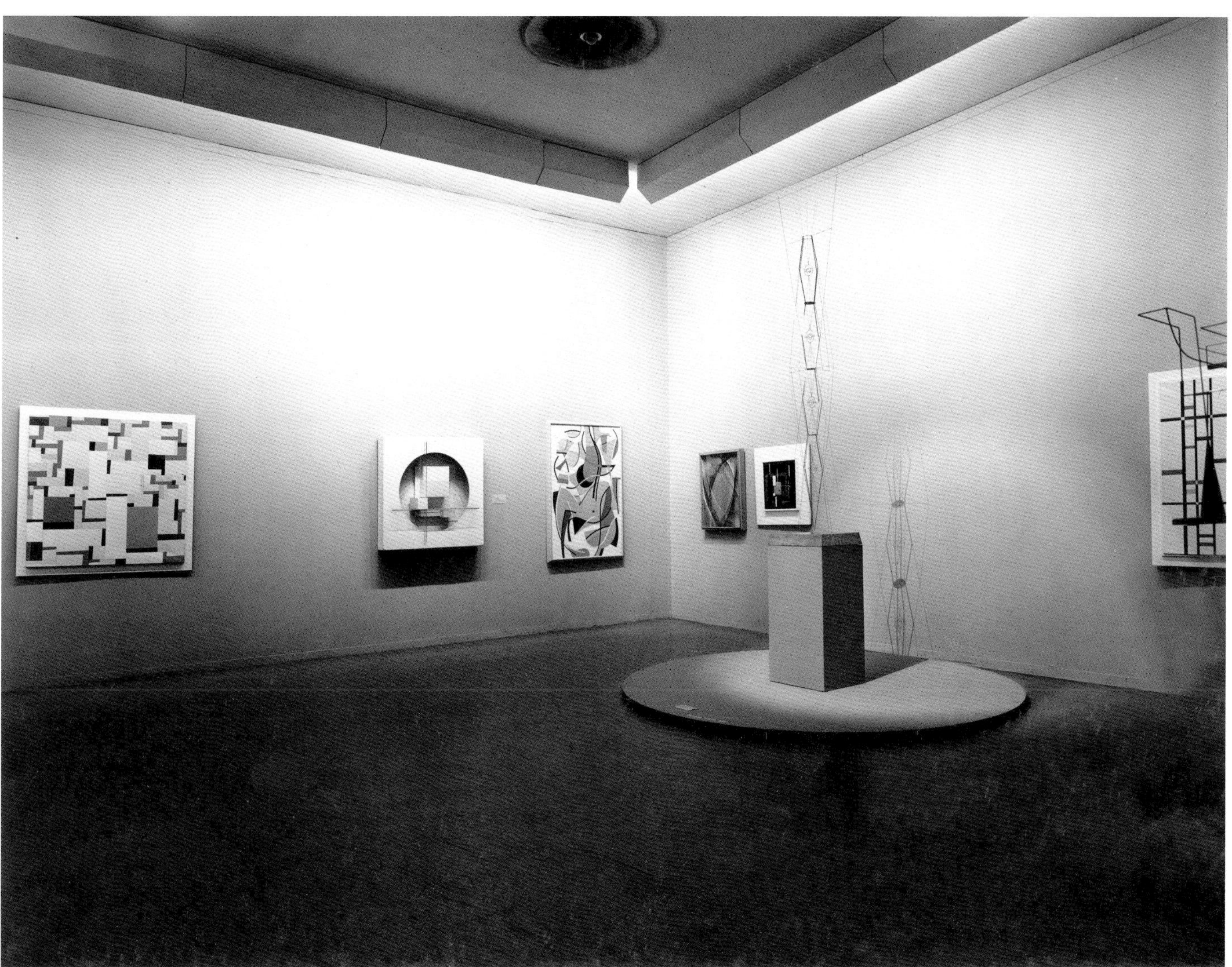

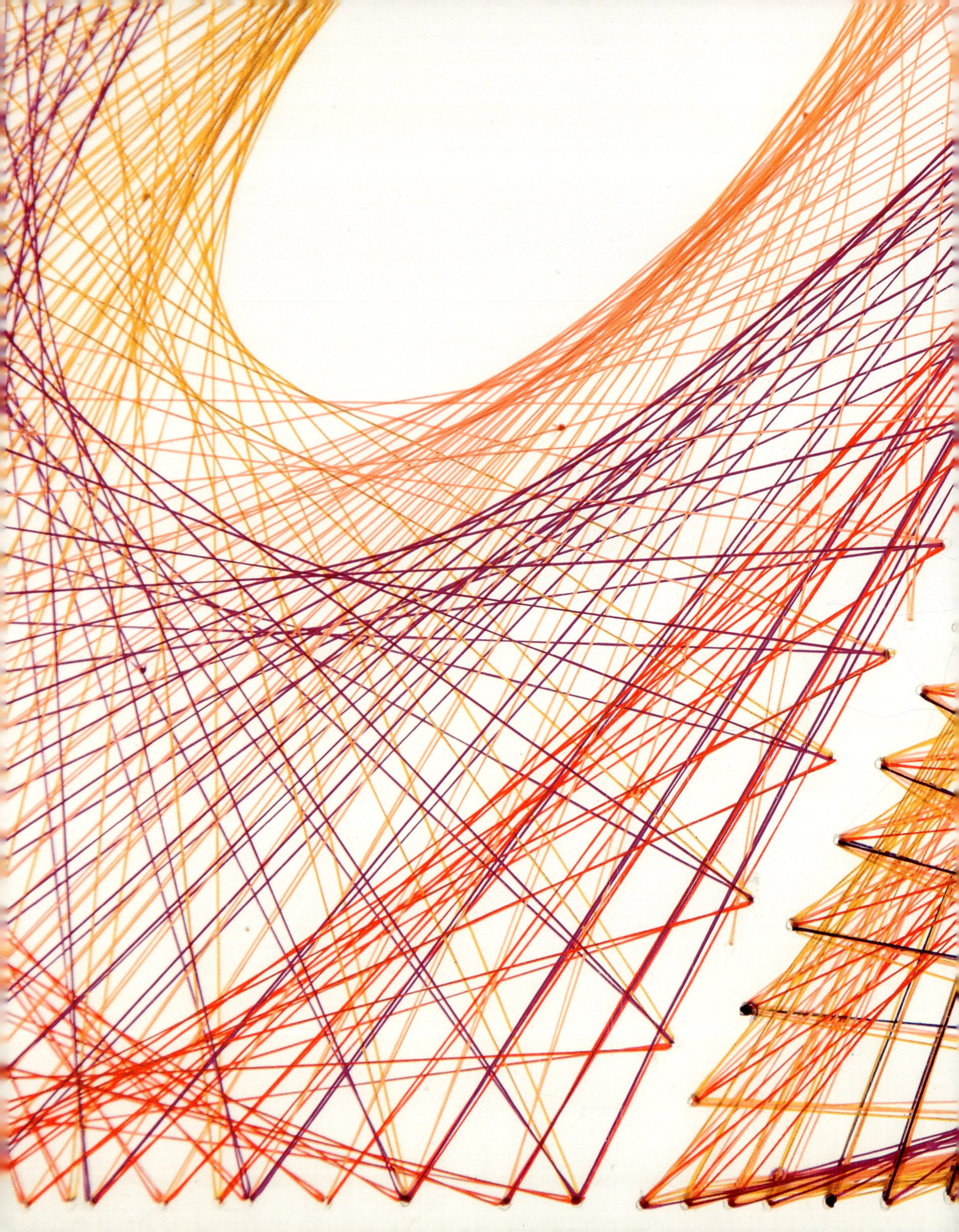

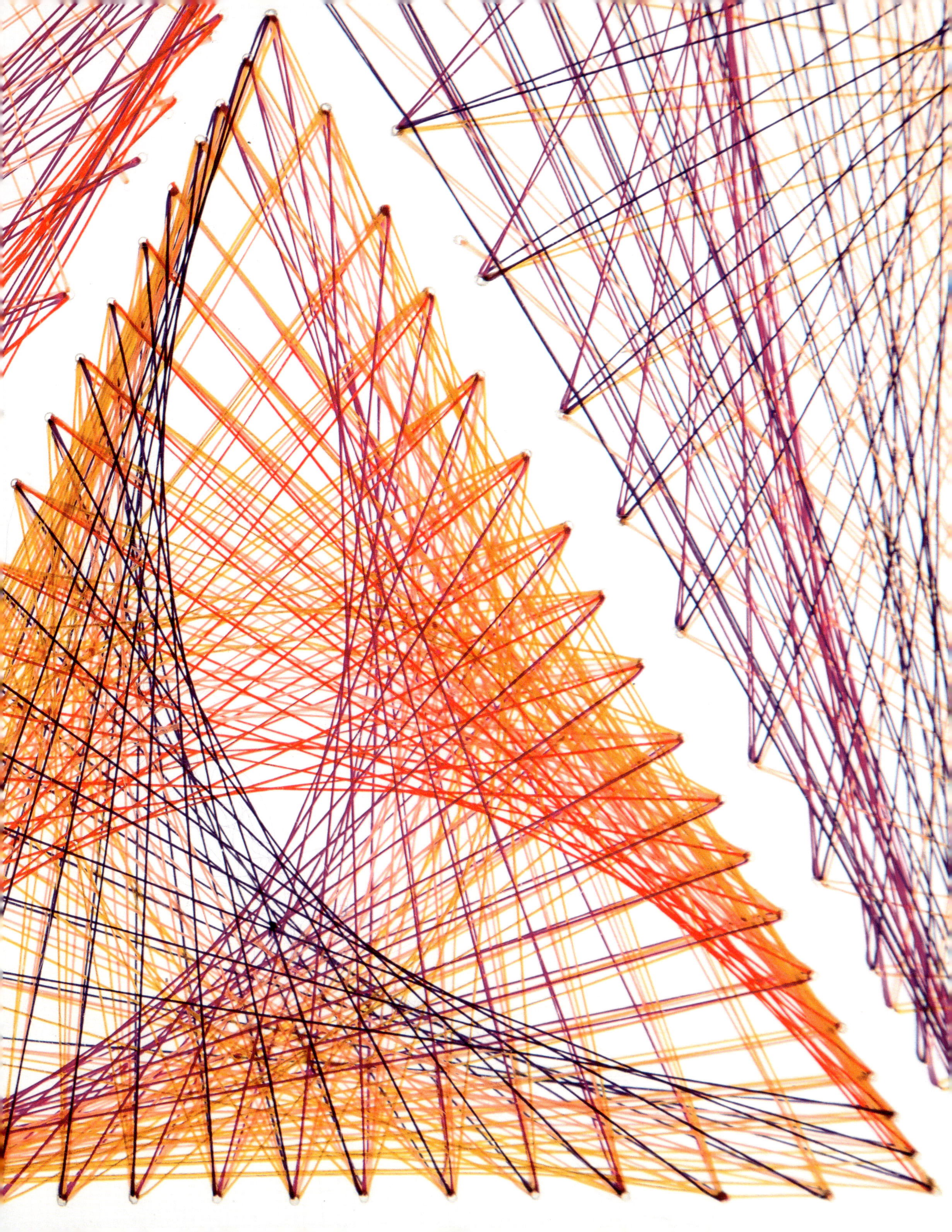

Sue Fuller's 'Know-How'

Alex J. Taylor

Fig.6
Sue Fuller, *String Composition #50*, 1952–53
Plastic thread, painted Masonite and aluminium frame
34 × 45 in. (86.4 × 114.3 cm)
The Metropolitan Museum of Art, New York

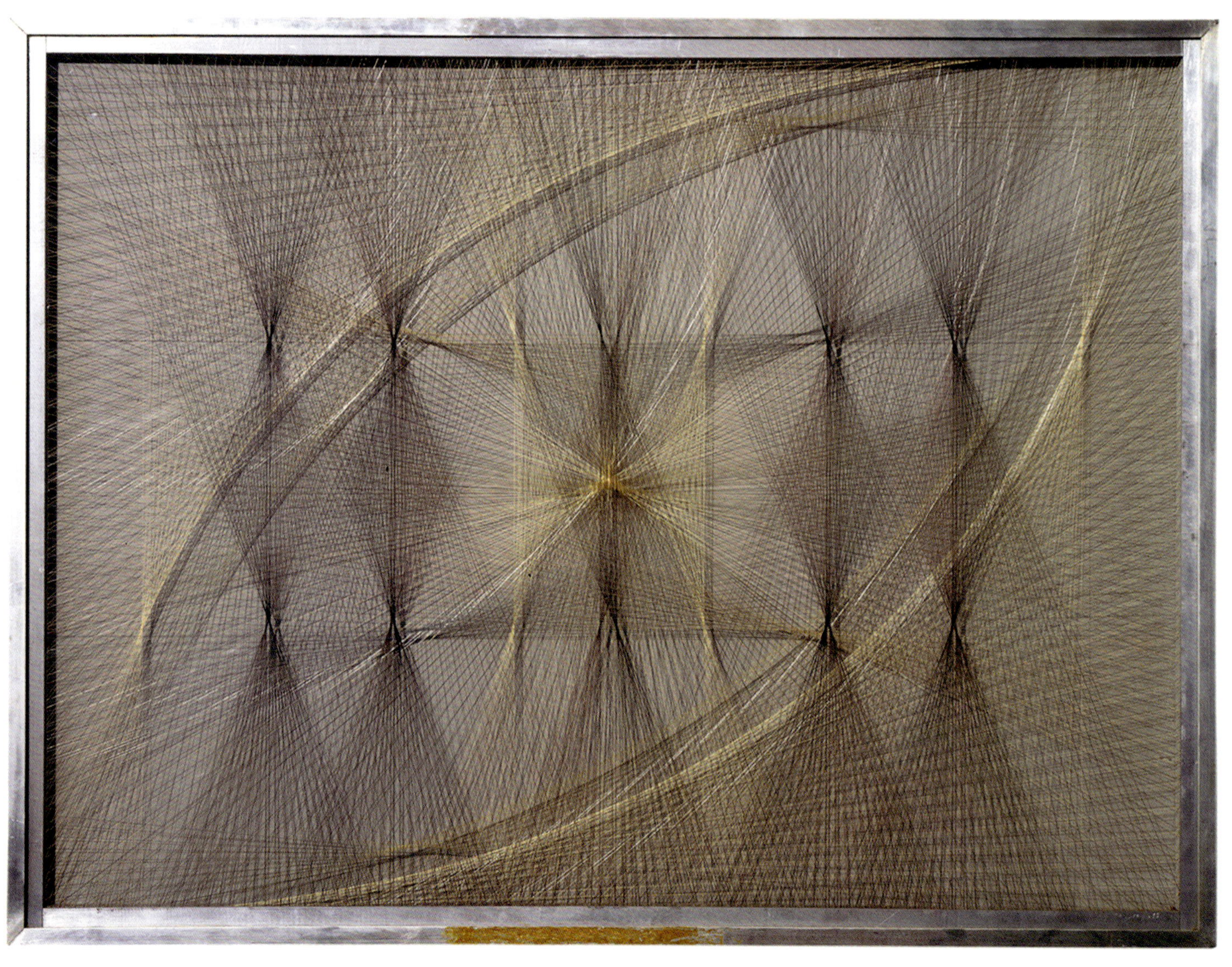

In November 1968, Sue Fuller was in Chicago to explore the future of plastics, the material upon which her art by then relied. The occasion was the National Plastics Exposition, a vast trade show and conference marking the 100th anniversary of the invention of celluloid. 'Today heard a session on furniture', she wrote to a friend. 'Boy! Talk about grape-nuts epoxy Spanish provincial! Yeow!'[1] Fuller's lively note registers the perils of her potentially low-brow material with a knowing wink. But the flipside of her correspondence simultaneously spoke of the material's more avant-garde possibilities. Picked up at the Art Institute of Chicago, her postcard reproduced a vibrant stained canvas by Jules Olitski, a painting made, not coincidentally, from one of the synthetic paints that had swept through artist studios in the late 1950s and early 1960s.

That is to say, both post-painterly abstraction and suburban breakfast room decor had been indelibly shaped by plastics. And Fuller knew, I think, that these seemingly separate spheres had more to do with each other than most recognised. At the risk of reading too much into this casual piece of correspondence, I want to consider how it suggests Fuller to have engaged the interconnections between modern abstract art and other kinds of manufactured goods, the uneasy but ultimately productive relations that dominant accounts of postwar art ordinarily disavow.[2] Fuller embraced these affinities through materials and techniques drawn from beyond the limits of fine art. Her drive to invent something new was as characteristically modernist as her enthusiasm for modernity itself was affirmative. But here I also want to examine how the sheer newness of her string compositions – the startlingly original creation that made her famous – saw Fuller tackle questions of originality and ownership head-on.

Within a decade of their first appearance in the late 1940s, Fuller's string compositions secured a place of their own in an emerging canon of American geometrical abstraction. This was an art, as critic Thomas Hess described Fuller and like-minded peers, defined by its 'native ingenuity ... inventiveness and skill – one is even tempted to call it "know-how"'.[3] Her inclusion in such landmark exhibitions as the Museum of Modern Art's *Abstract Painting and Sculpture in America* (1951, fig.5, p.9), curated by Andrew Carnduff Ritchie, and the Whitney Museum of American Art's touring exhibition *The New Decade: 35 American Painters and Sculptors* (1955) – both of which produced important publications through which reproductions of Fuller's work were circulated – would establish her string compositions within that brand of American modernism defined by its technical prowess and commitment to material innovation.[4] Subsequent acquisitions of major Fuller works for the collections of the Whitney Museum and the Metropolitan Museum of Art (fig.6) in the mid-1950s help confirm the serious recognition that her practice rapidly achieved.

But even before she embraced abstraction, we might detect more subtle signs of Fuller's orientation towards an imagery of material 'know-how'. In her early painting *Sonnenschein Umbrella Company* (1942), women are shown making umbrellas in a crowded, ramshackle sweatshop, a drab chamber that reinforces the irony of the fictional company's name, taken from the German word for 'sunshine'. Of the retracted constructions that hang from the rafters, collapsed antecedents of Fuller's sprawling geometries, one critic explained that they probably 'caught the artist's eye as might some gothic fretwork'.[5] There is indeed a grim, grey mood to this picture, but it also concerns the intricate handiwork required – then and now – to assemble a product from its component parts. It is surely prescient that, in the same review, the subject of this painting was described as merely that from which 'she spins her pattern', as though the social realist content of Fuller's early works was already subordinate to their underlying formal structure.[6]

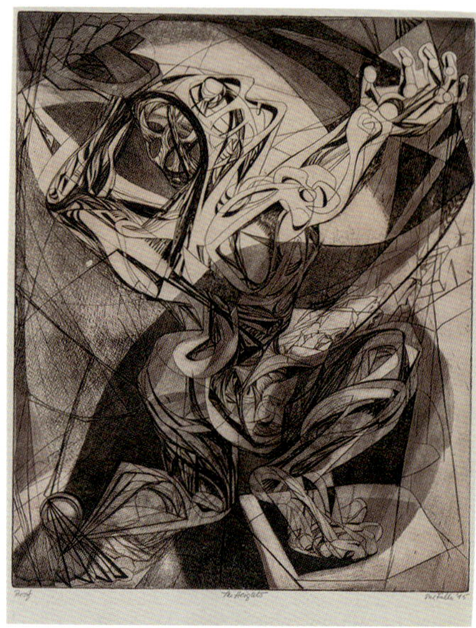

Fig.7
Sue Fuller, *The Heights*, 1945
Engraving and soft-ground etching on white wove paper
14¾ × 11⅞ in. (37.5 × 30.2 cm)

Moving to New York to first study and then work in Stanley William Hayter's Atelier 17, Fuller became an accomplished printmaker in the 1940s.[7] In *The Heights* (1945, fig.7), for instance, she renders an abstracted body whose very musculature appears to peel away into the striated, linear force of its energy. Fuller's figure gestures towards Picasso, but the underlying field of light and dark arcs bisected by linear trajectories is already distinctively her own. 'The figure struggling upward through a lavender maze of lines and netlike patterned ground', explained art historian and curator Virginia Lewis, 'might be symbolizing the supplication of the mechanical age – a begging for understanding of more than we, as limited human beings, can grasp in even our own rapid discoveries and accomplishments of recent years.'[8] This sense that Fuller's imagery dealt with technological change – the 'high-strung quality of this era', as Lewis later put it – was a recurring theme in the reception of her early prints.[9]

Fuller's incorporation of woven textiles into her printmaking practice quickly led to stand-alone experiments with string itself. In the late 1940s, such designs began to fill her studio, first taped to pieces of paper, later nailed to boards. Eventually Fuller came to understand these designs as finished works in their own right. 'I pulled or stretched them, reassembled them; then finally reduced their structure down to one thread', she later explained.[10] In early efforts such as *String Composition #12* (1948, fig.8), Fuller used geometrical fields as backgrounds for looser, figurative forms in string. But soon these figure–ground relationships disappeared. The result saw arrays of threads converging and separating like tiny beams of light or complex plotted graphs, extending the machine-age allusions in her prints to achieve an assured détente between the material traditions of the handmade and the invisible forces of technological modernity.

One source for Fuller's reduction 'down to one thread' was the joint retrospective of Naum Gabo and Antoine Pevsner that she saw in February 1948 (fig.9). 'I'd just seen Gabo and Pevsner in the Museum of Modern Art and the sight of all that string and Lucite overwhelmed me', she later recalled.[11] But Fuller was rather more playful in her material experimentation than such European émigré Constructivists, delighting in the sheer variety of threads at her disposal. Early works shuttled from 'gossamer silk, now to bright fuzzy wool, now to dull, natural cord, and

Fig.8
Sue Fuller, *String Composition #12*, 1948
Polypropylene thread, mixed media and fabric laid on canvas
25⅝ × 19½ × 3 in. (65 × 50 × 6.5 cm)

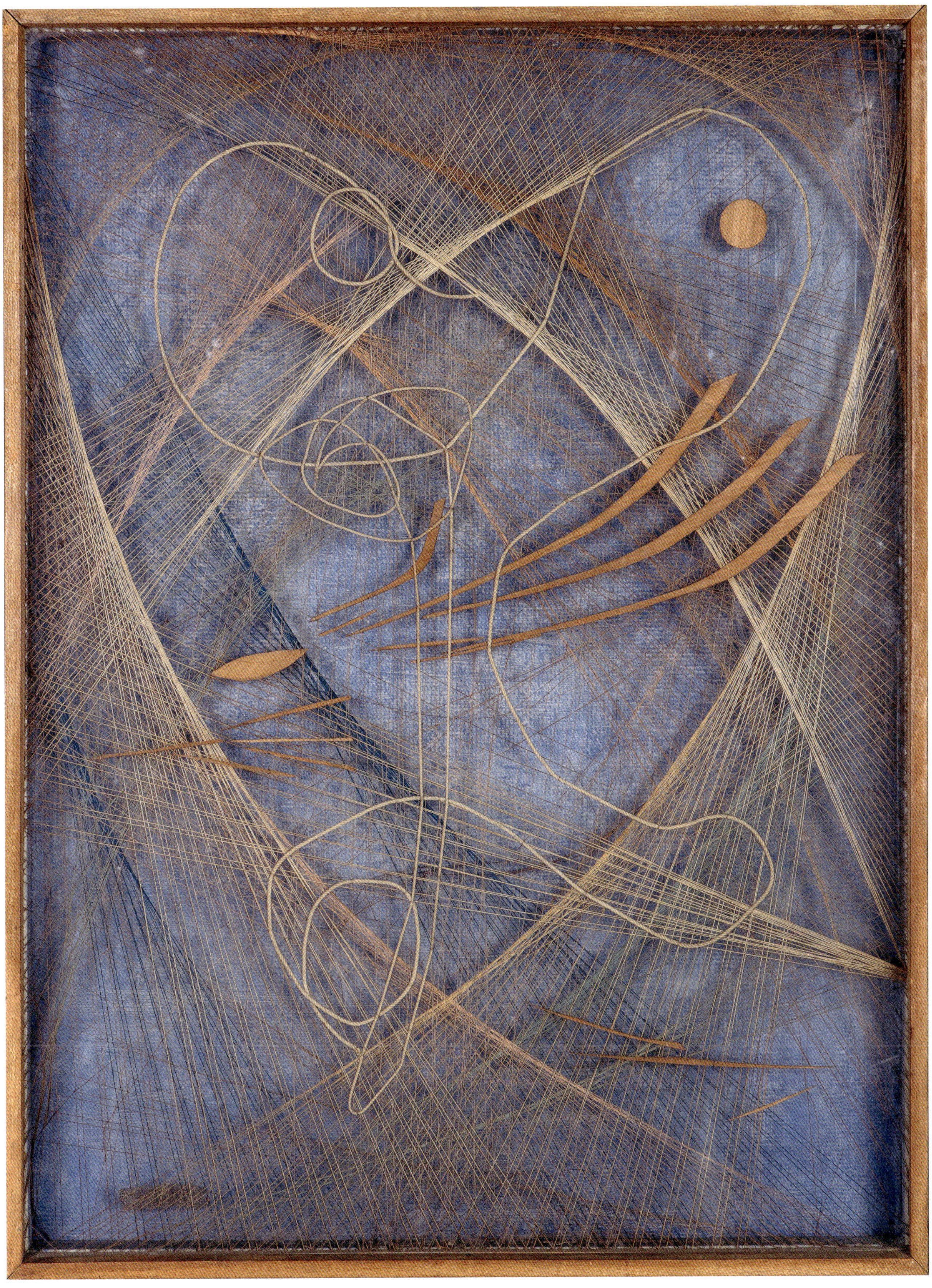

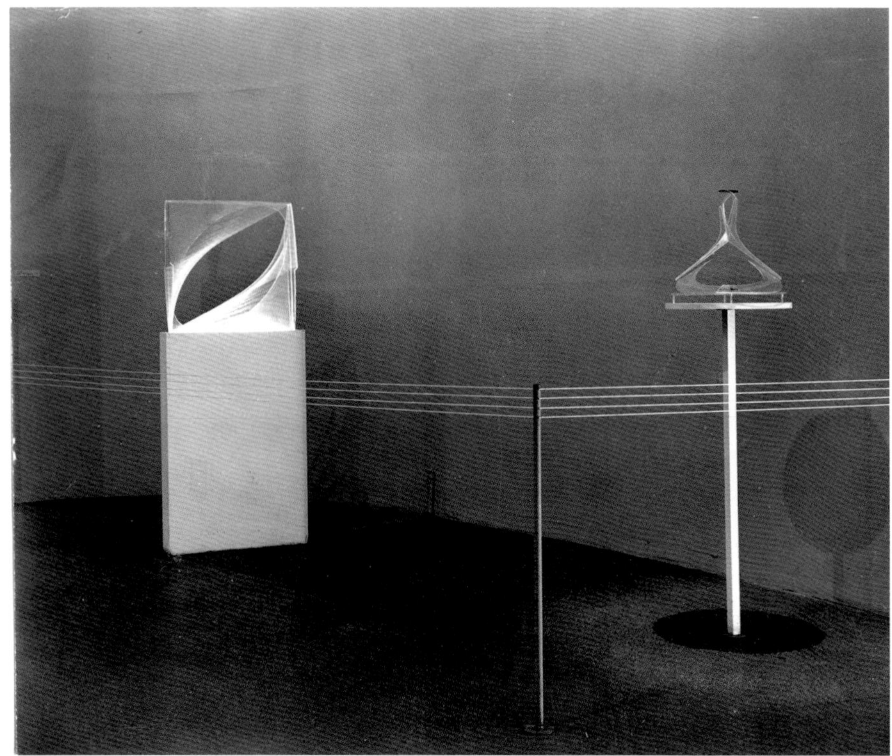

Fig.9
Installation view of the exhibition
Naum Gabo – Antoine Pevsner at the
Museum of Modern Art, New York, 1948

now to metallic string which sparkles and shimmers with a gaudy luster', as one critic described the works in her 1950 solo exhibition.[12] Fuller later admitted that these early string compositions used her material rather 'indiscriminately', and she quickly faced the realities of sagging threads and fading dyes. 'Then and there began the search for a more permanent palette of thread colors which also have no objectionable structural characteristics', explained critic Rosalind Browne.[13]

The first plastic thread Fuller discovered was in an insect screen bought from a hardware store.[14] Fuller initially focused on early synthetic fibres like rayon and nylon, but eventually came to prefer extruded thermoplastic monofilaments such as polyvinylidene chloride (PVDC) or polypropylene (PP) – which would not 'sag and tighten with changes in weather and humidity'.[15] Fuller also hired a machinist to fabricate her custom aluminium and brass frames, so essential to maintain the taut geometries of her works. 'I have a closet full of "learn by doing" attempts at framemaking', she later admitted.[16] Such technical investments were a bet on the future of her artworks. 'If your work is going to be found in a museum,' she told Browne, 'then the museum should have the guarantee that you've done your best to make it permanent.'[17] For Fuller, such responsibilities also concerned the artist's obligation to 'record your time', which is to say that she understood her material innovations to represent a lasting image of the present for the future.[18]

Fuller's long commitment to synthetic thread – as her presence at the Plastics Expo corroborates – was one that necessitated her ongoing involvement with industrial and scientific experts. Her engagement with industrial manufacturers appears to have been reciprocal from the very beginning. Her 1951 exhibition at the Corcoran Gallery of Art in Washington, DC included five works purchased by the Celanese Corporation, likely the works that one critic noted had 'been used by a big corporation for advertising display purposes'. Fuller's faith in the possibilities of corporate patronage lasted throughout her career. 'Industry has been backing artists and letting them do their own thing. It's one of the solutions for art today', she explained in 1972.[19] In line with such possibilities, Fuller frequently indicated the brand names of her materials, often favouring such proprietary designations over the more generic material names under which they are now usually exhibited.

By the mid-1950s, Fuller's practice brought together a rigorously non-objective but instantly recognisable trademark style. The result was some of her most accomplished constructions, crystalline geometries like *String Composition #68* (1955) and *String Composition #74* (1956). The refined abstraction of works like these should not distract from the rather more vernacular sources upon which they drew. As I have explored elsewhere, her research into the anthropology of string figures (such as the game 'cat's cradle') was one example of this, as was her exploration of lacemaking and sailing knots.[20] Such interests also extended beyond string. In 1951, for instance, Fuller went to the School of Arts and Crafts in the West Midlands town of Stourbridge, the historic centre of British glass-making, recognising that her work with string recalled some of the effects of caneworking, whereby long rods of glass are fused to produce intricately striped patterns.[21]

Another example of the exploratory approach that Fuller used to find sources for modernist abstraction is evident in her time in Japan, where she spent six months learning calligraphy with Teruo Tokuno in 1954. Upon her return to the United States, Fuller published an illustrated essay about her experiences.[22] Her text ranges across the social functions and material requirements of the art form, with long passages dealing with the particularities of brushes, ink and paper, and its varied display modes as a 'hanging scroll, a screen or a sliding door panel'. Above all, Fuller was impressed to note that Japanese calligraphers had, in her view, 'absorbed the modern art of other countries', with some of its leading practitioners having 'completely abandoned any visible trace of language or literary symbol'.[23] Fuller could not read Japanese, and so it was the 'fabulous juxtapositions of shapes in the characters' that necessarily excited her most – further evidence, for Fuller, of the universality of the abstract forms to which she was so committed.[24]

As should be clear, Fuller's interest in such sources tended to reinforce the cultural hierarchies typical of modernism's appetite for non-Western art. 'Since I was not an Eskimo, a Navaho Indian, or a South Sea Islander, but the product of a more complex culture pattern, my expression in string took on a different character', she explained in 1954. 'Inspired by the engineering genius of our times and civilization, expressed in transparency, light and balance, I found the form of lineal geometric progression more significant for this expression of thought.'[25] For Fuller, and despite her engagement in the social histories of the visual and material cultures she explored, it was abstraction that was best suited to capture the experience of modern industrial civilisation. 'Though I fully appreciated the products of the engineer – airplanes, bridges, skyscrapers – mere representation of these symbols was not enough to convey my feeling.'[26]

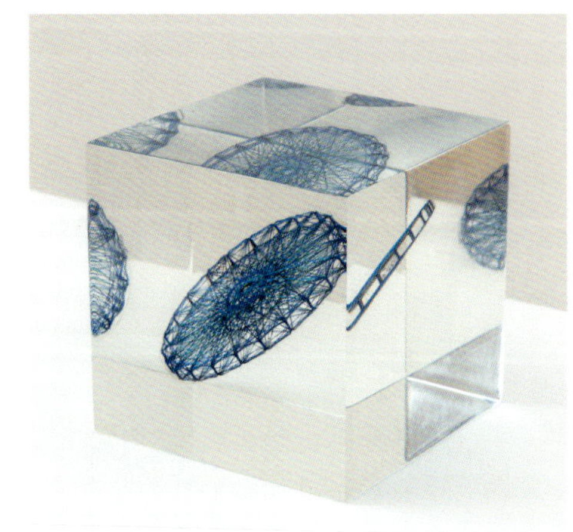

Fig.10
Sue Fuller, *String Composition #408*, 1965
Lucite and polypropylene thread
5¾ × 5¾ × 5¾ in. (14.5 × 14.5 × 14.5 cm)

In 1968, as Fuller mingled with the delegates at Chicago's Plastics Expo, she might well have discussed her enthusiasm for the 'products of the engineer' or her career-long experimentation with materials sourced from beyond the art supply store. Some of those at the conference might even have known her work from *Plastics USA*, the touring exhibition sent by the United States Information Agency to the Soviet Bloc in the early 1960s, a 450-square-metre display of everyday plastic objects seen by almost 1 million visitors.[27] But, by the late 1960s, a more likely subject for her discussions was her visions for the future – in particular, I suspect, the artistic invention that was the subject of her pending application to the United States Patent Office.

In early 1965, Fuller hired an attorney to help her secure exclusive rights to an invention that gave her string compositions a new and more sculptural spin. As her patent application explains, the idea was to compose her designs in thread across the notched edges of a hard acrylic panel, and then immerse the composition in a mould of liquid plastic. Once set, 'since the matrix and panel materials are identically transparent or translucent ... the viewer is unable to optically distinguish there-between', reads the patent application. Eliminating the need for a frame, the technique allowed Fuller to further breach the borders between two- and three-dimensional art and produce a composition, as her documentation claims, 'free of aesthetic interference'.[28]

The result was string compositions embedded within a block of clear plastic, like a snowflake caught in a permanent state of suspension. One writer thought they looked like 'bananas in jello', but given Fuller's interest in glass-making, they more precisely recall the intricate microcosms of nineteenth-century French glass paperweights, like crystal balls remade for the hard-edged modularity of the modern age.[29] *String Composition #408* (1965, fig.10) is an early example of the technique, its circular form shifting dramatically as one views its web through different aspects of the plastic that encases it. As Fuller explained of a related work from the same year, *String Composition #333* (1965, pp.46–47), 'it is a translucent drawing in blue and green threads apparently suspended in a crystal-clear transparent block. When properly displayed it appears to be a drawing in green and blue light.'[30] The effect, she noted, 'took me twenty years of work and research to produce'.[31]

Fuller's patent was finally granted on 24 June 1969 (fig.11). Her action was relatively unique among modern artists. Yves Klein had registered the process of making his trademark blue but did not apply for a patent as is sometimes claimed.[32] Sculptor Kenneth Snelson is a more comparable instance, significant for the formal language of suspension that also characterised his constructions of tubular aluminium and steel wire. 'What I have done in the patent is to fully describe how my sculpture is composed, what it is that makes it work', he told critic John Coplans. 'If anyone wants to use it I am not going to stop them.'[33] In one unpublished interview, Fuller told curator Elayne Varian – by contrast – that she did 'not want to stifle' popular interest in her art, but that she also wished for her work to be treated 'on the same basis as an inventor and should be protected and paid'.[34] Fuller's patent was not just a matter of validating the originality of art, it was about defending her practice from commercial imitation from which someone else sought to profit.

It is therefore no accident that Fuller lodged the application in February 1965, two weeks before her work was about to be included in *The Responsive Eye* exhibition at the Museum of Modern Art. Fuller was, to be sure, a tangential figure in this celebrated survey of Op art by the likes of Bridget Riley and Richard Anuszkiewicz.[35] But even before this exhibition opened, insiders predicted that it would spur a flood of mass-produced imitations. 'Optical art is this year's dress length', reported *Time* magazine in October 1964.[36] Art collector and fashion designer Larry Aldrich took the news literally, using a Riley canvas he owned as the basis for a printed fabric and surprising the artist with an impromptu fashion show. As others have recounted, the artist was furious. 'Nobody even asked my permission', Riley told an interviewer.[37]

Fig.11
Sue Fuller, Technique for Producing String Compositions, United States Patent No.3,451,879, patented 24 June 1969

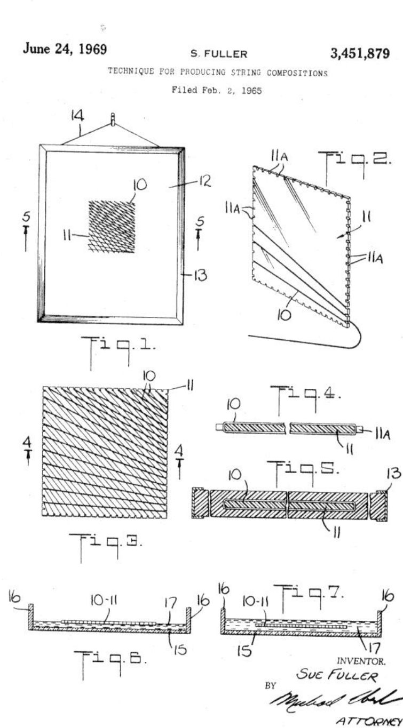

The more complex and subtle materiality of Fuller's constructions – works that have always been challenging to photograph and reproduce – probably protected her from such copies (fig.12). And yet Riley's predicament was one that Fuller understood all too well. The first imitations of her art had appeared, innocuously enough, in the sphere of arts education. In the pages of *School Arts*, a periodical for art teachers to which Fuller herself contributed, string compositions stretched across frames began to be suggested as a classroom activity for students.[38] In one 1957 article, for instance, Fuller was named as the 'inspiration' for the work of a sixth-grade class. The article illustrates the class making string designs across wooden frames, much like Fuller's early efforts, and describes how these students had experienced the 'high pitch of creative excitement that can only come when suddenly one realizes the uncommon aesthetic possibilities in a seemingly banal material'.[39]

I think Fuller would have understood the ramifications of such imitations, a development at once flattering and worrying. She had played a modest role in helping to spur the diffusion of mobiles made in the style of Alexander Calder as the instructor for the 'Experiments in Mobile Design' school programme at the Museum of Modern Art in 1947.[40] And something of the same fate lay ahead for Fuller. In the early 1970s, simplified versions of her techniques would become a mainstay of the commercial craft

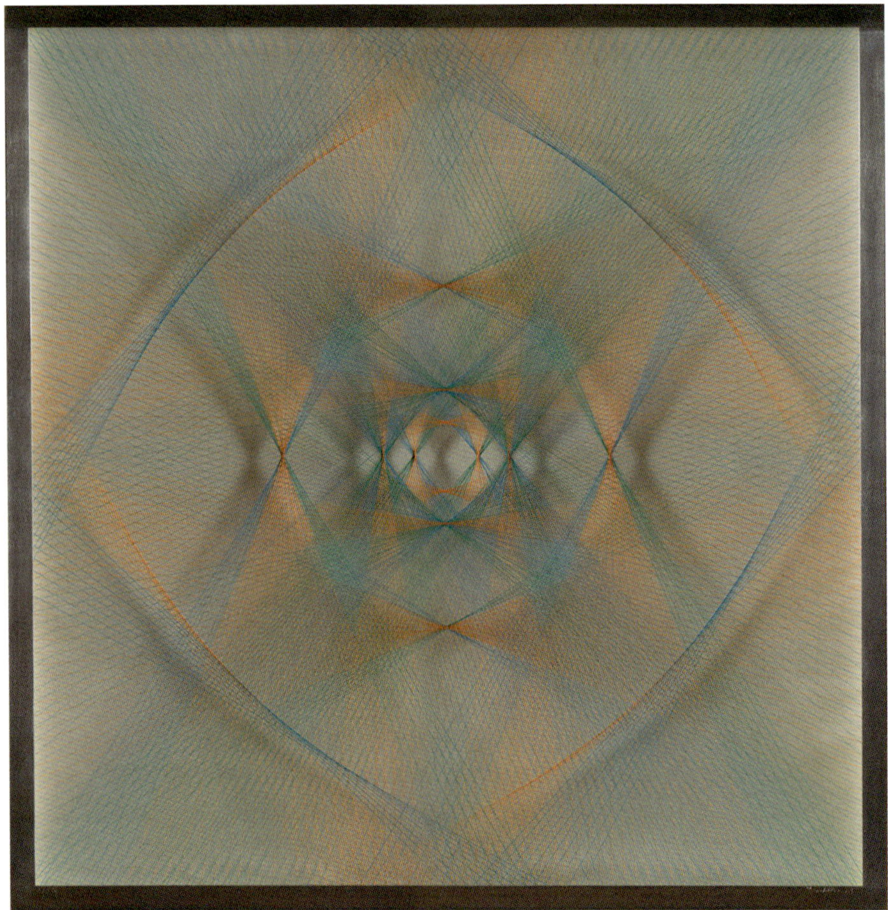

Fig.12
Sue Fuller, *String Composition #128*, 1964
Construction of polypropylene thread with wood, cloth and integral metal frame
36 × 36 × 1½ in. (91.5 × 91.5 × 4 cm)
Tate, London

industry. Prefabricated kits and pattern books flourished, many referring to the art as 'symmography', a term that seems to have been invented by author Lois Kreischer for her best-selling 1971 craft book. This paperback reportedly sold some 200,000 copies – and fails to mention Fuller once.[41] A subsequent book by Laura Sarff and Jan Harem titled *Symmography: Linear Thread Design* (1979) was more generous to the art form's originator, illustrating several Fuller works (including her most recent 'plastic embedments') with the artist's permission.[42]

Fuller later acknowledged such imitations. 'Some schmucks have been ripping me off – but that's par for the course', she wrote in a 1978 letter.[43] But it is noteworthy that Fuller seems to have already experimented with the idea of creating kits that would allow her techniques to be executed by others. In the papers of Fuller's friend Florence Forst, one 1960 image is marked to be a work made 'from the directions written up by Sue Fuller'.[44] A handwritten note appears to detail the notion of developing a 'kit' by which others could fabricate her designs. Forst's husband, an engineer at 3M, suggested 'direction revisions' such as using 'the word "slot" instead of "groove"' and including 'more complete labeling, [and] more directional arrows'.[45] The idea seems not to have been pursued, but, alongside her patent registration later in the decade, it suggests that Fuller was attentive to both the perils and possibilities of her practice in the sphere of mass consumption.

Another example helps capture the coexistence of such seemingly contradictory impulses. In December 1955, Fuller's art was on display at the Los Angeles County Museum of Art as part of *The New Decade*, the Whitney Museum's landmark survey of postwar American art, alongside Willem de Kooning and Jackson Pollock, but also other now neglected artists whose focus on material 'know-how' was more closely tuned to Fuller's, like Leo Amino and Richard Lippold. The same month, Fuller's rather less abstract 'paper sculptures' of the Twelve Days of Christmas could be seen on the front cover of the Christmas issue of *Better Homes and Gardens*. The magazine contained templates for copying her intricately cut and folded designs.[46] The issue also featured a design by Fuller for a suspended floor-to-ceiling construction billed as a room divider or 'conversation piece', a kind of skeletal *Endless Column* in yarn.[47]

Fuller's position between the spheres of high modernism and interior decor was, I think, fundamental to her practice, and was reflected in the approach of her dealer Bertha Schaefer, who straddled the same boundaries. 'Miss Schaefer is defying a traditional though artificial enmity between the "fine" and "applied" arts', a journalist noted in 1957. 'She has not always escaped with impunity.'[48] Such critical alignments were inevitably gendered, and sometimes pejoratively so, but they ultimately represented – as art historian Susan Richmond has noted of the collages of Anne Ryan, another Hayter alumnus – 'an embodied intelligence that drifted from the "ordinary" modalities of the domestic to the "extraordinary" realm of art'.[49] Fuller's consistent engagement with materials and techniques beyond the sphere of fine art cultivated her own ease with an equally liminal position. Because what these explorations revealed was that the idea of an autonomous avant-garde defined by originality was a fiction – even for an artist whose inventions were as unequivocally original as Fuller's, and even given her desire to exercise a modicum of control over her inventions and profit from the products of her creative labour.

'Art has always belonged to all peoples of all times and includes all mediums', Fuller explained in a 1954 article. Her explorations of both new materials and traditional crafts had, she wrote, 'opened my eyes to see and appreciate that which mankind had already accomplished in related fields'. This was not a matter of 'merely copying or imitating what had been done before, but was discovery based on an understanding exploration of the materials and methods'.[50] A later statement further reiterated such perspectives. 'Where there are no rules or directions, yours is the responsibility to search them out for yourself', she noted. 'What happens is, that you do something which makes everybody aware of what has been here all along.'[51] Fuller's modernism was one in which she sought out new discoveries – but was never arrogant enough to imagine that her 'know-how' existed apart from all the other kinds of creative invention that surround us every day.

1 The painting on the postcard is Olitski's *Born in Snovsk* (1962). Sue Fuller, postcard to Ed and Florence Forst, 14 November 1968, Sue Fuller letters to Florence Forst, 1950–1994, Archives of American Art, Smithsonian Institution, Washington, DC.
2 See, most famously, Clement Greenberg, 'Avant Garde and Kitsch', in *Art and Culture: Critical Essays*, Beacon Press, Boston, 1961, pp.3–21.
3 Thomas Hess, 'Is Abstraction Un-American?' *Art News*, vol.49, no.10, February 1951, p.40.
4 See Andrew Carnduff Ritchie, *Abstract Painting and Sculpture in America*, exhibition catalogue, Museum of Modern Art, New York, 1951, p.84, and John I.H. Baur, *The New Decade: 35 American Painters and Sculptors*, exhibition catalogue, Whitney Museum of American Art, New York, 1955, pp.27–29.
5 Jeanette Jena, 'Associated Artists Present Mild, But Easy to Look at Show', *Pittsburgh Post-Gazette*, 13 February 1942, p.6.
6 *Ibid.*
7 On Fuller's prints, see Christina Weyl, *The Women of Atelier 17: Modernist Printmaking in Midcentury New York*, Yale University Press, New Haven, CT, 2019.
8 Virginia Lewis, 'Current American Artists', *Carnegie Magazine*, December 1945, p.173.
9 Virginia Lewis, 'This Year's Crop of Prints', *Carnegie Magazine*, December 1947, p.132.
10 Fuller quoted in Rosalind Browne, 'Sue Fuller: Threading Transparency', *Art International*, January 1972, p.39.
11 Fuller quoted *ibid.*, p.38.
12 B.K. [Belle Krasne], 'Fuller: Advantage of String', *Art Digest*, vol.24, no.18, July 1950, p.19.
13 Browne, *op. cit.*, p.39.
14 *String Compositions by Sue Fuller: Transparency, Light and Balance*, unidentified exhibition catalogue, unpaginated, Sue Fuller letters to Florence Forst, *op. cit.* In her statement in Claude Marks, *World Artists, 1950–1980*, H.W. Wilson, New York, 1984, p.295, Fuller mentions experimenting with the products of company Chicopee Mills, who produced screen doors using Owens-Corning Fibreglas (see 'New Fibreglas Screening!', *Life*, 11 April 1955, p.135).
15 Thelma R. Newman, *Plastics as an Art Form*, Chilton Books, Philadelphia PA, 1964, p.225.
16 *String Compositions by Sue Fuller*, *op. cit.*, n.p.
17 Fuller quoted in Browne, *op. cit.*, p.38.
18 *Ibid.*
19 *Ibid.*
20 See Alex J. Taylor, 'Common Threads', in Alex J. Taylor, Christina Weyl and Frances Follin, '*String Composition 128* (1964) by Sue Fuller', Tate Research Publication, 2018, www.tate.org.uk/research/in-focus/string-composition-128, accessed 2 August 2022.
21 Fuller may well have known of the school from accounts of the career of Frederick Carder (1863–1963), who was born in Staffordshire, England, and later co-founded the Steuben Glass Works in Corning, New York. Carder was the Stourbridge School's most prominent graduate in the United States. Fuller later remembered a piece of Venetian *latticino* glass owned by her father, and shared memories of the iridescent effects of the fancy leaded windows in her childhood home in Pittsburgh's East End. Fuller quoted in Browne, *op. cit.*, p.38.
22 Sue Fuller, 'The Art of Calligraphy: A Japanese Artist and His Tradition', *Arts Magazine*, August 1955, pp.8–11.
23 *Ibid.*, p.11.
24 Fuller quoted in Browne, *op. cit.*, p.38.
25 Sue Fuller, 'Twentieth Century Cat's Cradle', *Craft Horizons*, vol.14, no.2, April 1954, p.24.
26 *Ibid.*, p.24.
27 On this exhibition, see Tomas Tolvaisas, 'America on Display: United States Commercial and Cultural Exhibitions in the Soviet Bloc Countries, 1961–1968', PhD dissertation, Rutgers, The State University of New Jersey, 2007.
28 S. Fuller, 'Technique for Producing String Compositions', United States Patent 3,451,879, filed 2 February 1965, issued 24 June 1969. Elsewhere, Fuller notes the that 'Roy Stipp of Clearfloat, Inc. Atteboro' manufactured her first embedded works, and that 'as the capacity of the plant grew, so the size of the work I sent them increased'. Marks, *op. cit.*, p.295.
29 Browne, *op. cit.*, p.39.
30 *String Compositions by Sue Fuller*, *op. cit.*, n.p.
31 *Ibid.*
32 See Sophie Cras, *The Artist as Economist: Art and Capitalism in the 1960s*, Yale University Press, New Haven, CT, 2019. For more recent examples of this phenomenon, see Robert Thrill, 'Intellectual Property: A Chronological Compendium of Intersections Between Contemporary Art and Utility Patents', *Leonardo*, vol.37, no.2, 2004, pp.117–24.
33 John Coplans, 'An Interview with Kenneth Snelson', *Artforum*, March 1967, p.49.
34 Elayne Varian, 'Interview with Sue Fuller', unpublished transcript, Box 6, Folder 7, Exhibition Records of the Contemporary Wing of the Finch College Museum of Art, 1943–1975, Archives of American Art, Smithsonian Institution, Washington, DC.
35 Frances Follin, 'Unravelling Op', in Taylor, Weyl and Follin, *op. cit.*
36 Carl J. Weinhardt Jr quoted in 'Op Art: Pictures that Attack the Eye', *Time*, 23 October 1964, p.78.
37 For a useful account of this fracas, see Pamela Lee, *Chronophobia: On Time in the Art of the 1960s*, MIT Press, Cambridge, MA, pp.167–70.
38 Among the earliest examples is Jessie Todd, 'String Design', *School Arts*, June 1953, pp.334–35.
39 Fred R. Schwartz, 'Designs with Strings Attached', *School Arts*, November 1957, pp.23–24.
40 'Museum of Modern Art Shows Experiments in Mobile Design', *New York Herald Tribune*, 15 January 1947, p.16. On this fad, see Alex J. Taylor, 'The Calder Problem: Mobiles, Modern Taste, and Mass Culture', *Oxford Art Journal*, vol.37, no.1, March 2014, pp.27–45.
41 Lois Kreischer, *String Art: Symmography*, Crown, New York, 1971.
42 Laura Sarff and Jan Harem, *Symmography: Linear Thread Design*, Davis Publications, Worcester, MA, 1979.
43 Sue Fuller, letter to Florence Forst, 24 May 1978, Sue Fuller letters to Florence Forst, *op. cit.*
44 Note on reverse of unnamed photograph stamped 'Photographed by Grechen Studio', Sue Fuller letters to Florence Forst, *op. cit.*
45 'Sue Fuller's String Kits', handwritten note, undated, Sue Fuller letters to Florence Forst, *op. cit.*
46 'Twelve Days of Christmas', *Better Homes and Gardens*, December 1955, cover story, p.16.
47 'Here's a real conversation piece...', *Better Homes and Gardens*, December 1955, pp.61, 144.
48 'Case of Ambidexterity: Bertha Schaefer', *Interiors*, April 1957, pp.94–97.
49 Susan Richmond, 'The Craft of Anne Ryan's Collages', *Art History*, vol.44, no.1, February 2021, p.75.
50 Fuller, 'Twentieth Century Cat's Cradle', *op. cit.*, p.24.
51 *String Compositions by Sue Fuller*, *op. cit.*, n.p.

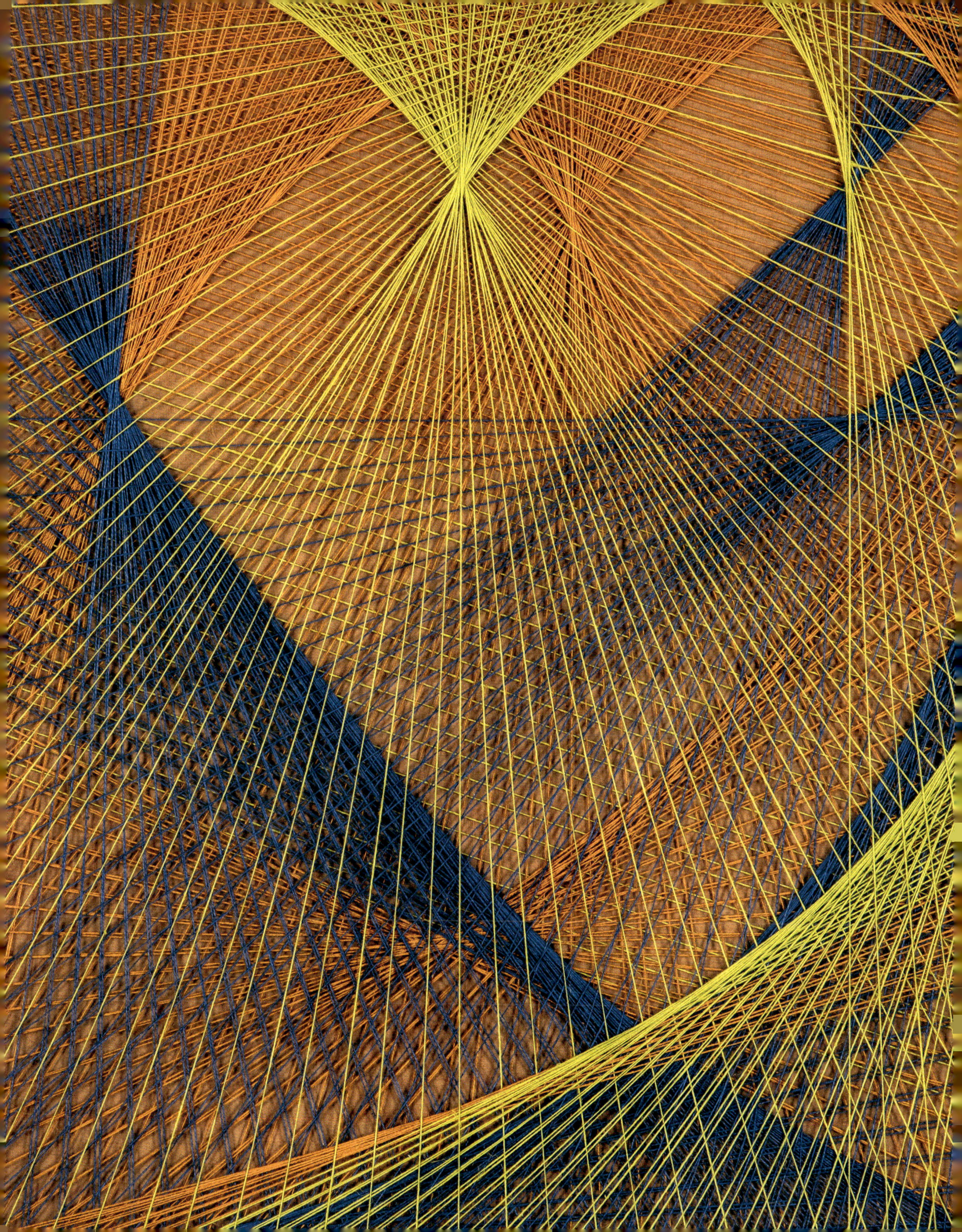

Sue Fuller: 'A New Poetry of Infinity'

Christina Weyl

Fig.13
Sue Fuller, c.1950
Photograph by Eileen Darby

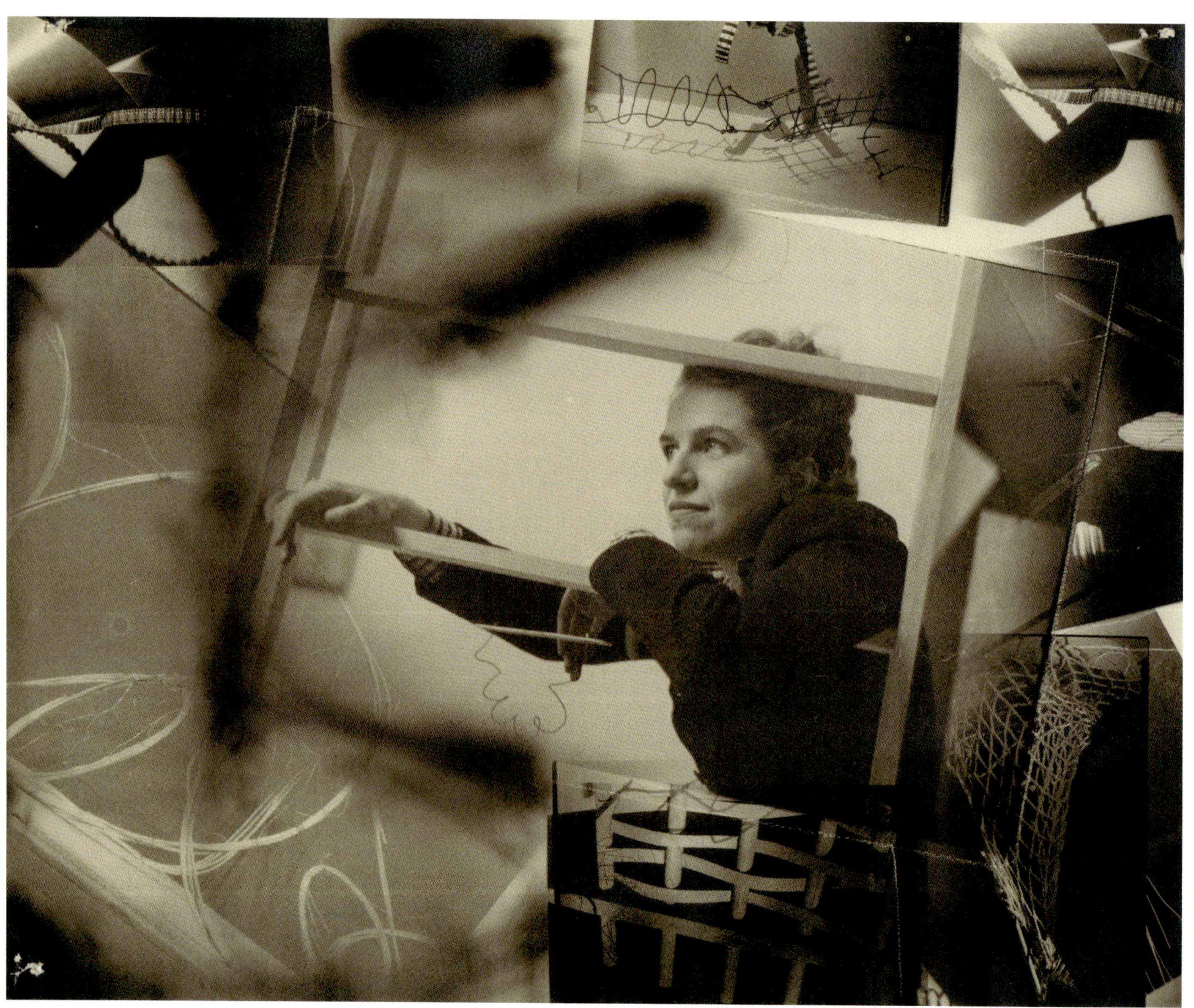

In 1948, Sue Fuller became the fortunate recipient of a Guggenheim Fellowship, the second of three prestigious grants she earned over a four-year period, the others endowed by the Louis Comfort Tiffany Foundation (1947) and the National Institute of Arts and Letters (1950). The Guggenheim grant came at a fulcrum in Fuller's career, just as she was accelerating her dedication to full-time work as a professional artist and beginning to make her signature string compositions.[1] Her proposed project, however, was born out of the graphic arts: Fuller had become increasingly fascinated with printmaking between 1944 and 1946 as a member of Atelier 17, the avant-garde printmaking workshop.[2] During the Guggenheim grant period, she envisioned a plan to enamel etched and engraved copper plates, following the medieval and Renaissance practices of *champlevé* and *basse-taille*. Ultimately, however, Fuller used her award to research the technique behind Mary Cassatt's etchings and write an influential article about them, which she published in *Magazine of Art*.[3]

As tangential as enamelling on copper or Mary Cassatt's nineteenth-century etchings may sound to Fuller's fibre-wrapped, geometric constructions, the Guggenheim project and supporting application materials hold significant clues to understanding the artist's approach to art-making and her philosophy about the purpose of her string compositions. Her application file at the Guggenheim Foundation provides a front-row seat to the inner workings of Fuller's mind: her inquisitive nature, her passion for research and zeal for continuous learning, her sense of humour and her adventurous spirit.[4] Most of all, Fuller makes clear in her statements the extent to which her artistic outlook was indebted to progressive philosophies of art education and to the principles developed at the Bauhaus, particularly its expansive approach to materials and effort to engage with viewers.

This framework, encompassing progressive education and the Bauhaus, has been missing from most discussion of Fuller's string compositions. Scholarly efforts to categorise Fuller's string compositions have proved elusive; the works are chameleon-like and nothing really seems to stick. These pieces are technically complicated and required Fuller to spend years researching component parts and strategies for fabrication.[5] Her intense focus on technique and craft put her on the outskirts of Greenbergian aesthetics and modernism, a point that art historian Jeffrey Saletnik has similarly made regarding the somewhat muted success of Bauhaus objects and pedagogical approaches in the United States.[6] In contrast, the printmaking community welcomed Fuller's technical prowess. During her lifetime she was seen as an expert and an important contributor to the expansion of the graphic arts at mid-century.

Within one year of receiving the Guggenheim Fellowship, Fuller exhibited the first group of nine string compositions – including *String Composition #12* (1948, fig.8, p.15), there titled sparsely *Twelve* – in a duo show with painter Peter Busa at Bertha Schaefer Gallery, New York. The gallery's press release states that the string compositions 'are conceived two-dimensionally as a collage'.[7] This early categorisation flows naturally from Fuller's approach to printmaking at Atelier 17.[8] At this esteemed printmaking studio, located in New York City between 1940 and 1955 following its relocation from Paris, members were encouraged to experiment with innovative techniques and make novel discoveries. Among other contributions, Fuller conceived an expansive approach to soft-ground etching, an intaglio process whereby the ground laid over the metal plate remains sticky due to the addition of wax or grease. Anything that touches the soft ground – such as handprints, botanical materials or fabric – pulls away the sticky resist and exposes the plate underneath to acid bite. Although Stanley William Hayter, Atelier 17's founder, encouraged studio members to employ soft-ground etching as tone and shadow to support etched or engraved line, Fuller saw more expansive potential for the technique.[9] In works such as *Hen* (1944, fig.14), she cut and reshaped a Victorian lace collar into the body of a chicken. As her experiments progressed, she grew frustrated with the limitations of stretching prefabricated material and wondered about 'reducing material to its least common denominator – a *string* and making my own *material*'.[10] For these abstract and semi-abstract prints, such as *Concerto* (1944), she would stretch, knot, twist and weave threads of different weights in order to create a collage that she would impress into the soft-grounded plate (fig.15).

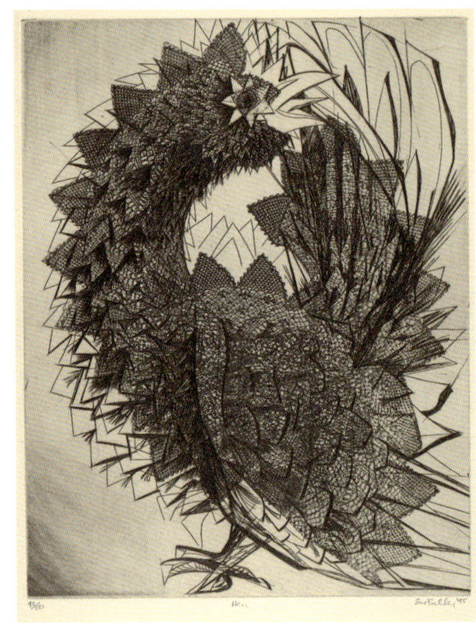

Fig.14
Sue Fuller, *Hen*, 1945
Soft-ground etching and engraving
19⅞ × 16 in. (50.5 × 40.7 cm)
The Metropolitan Museum of Art, New York (Purchase, Derald H. and Janet Ruttenberg Gift, 1994)

Fascinatingly, Fuller retroactively identified these soft-ground etchings and their preparatory collages as 'early string compositions', as described in a 1963 application to the Guggenheim Foundation for a renewal of her fellowship.[11] Hindsight makes it easy to see a formal lineage between Fuller's string compositions and the preparatory collages, many of which she kept as teaching tools or for exhibition. Some of the early stand-alone string compositions, such as *String Composition #12*, even have 'collaged' elements like the rambling, thick string and geometric shapes cut from matboard that are woven into the tension threads – not 'collaged' with glue in the strictest sense of the root French verb, *coller*. Identifying the string compositions as 'collages', however, proved unsuccessful, and Fuller appears to have dropped the label quickly.

The Guggenheim application materials provide a new framework for situating Fuller's string compositions within her background in art education, both as a student and an instructor, and her appreciation for Bauhaus-inspired principles regarding light, material and craft. On paper, Fuller did not have a direct connection to the Bauhaus or its instructors – or even the reconstitution of the Bauhaus in the United States at institutions such as Black Mountain College in North Carolina or the New Bauhaus in Chicago.[12] But she revered Josef and Anni Albers – each for different reasons – and clamoured for the opportunity to connect with them once the couple arrived in America. Early in her tenure as an art educator at the Museum of Modern Art during the late 1940s, Fuller attended a workshop with Josef Albers – a special offering organised by Victor D'Amico, her boss at the MoMA department of education.[13] Watching Albers teach that morning, Fuller realised that, to be an effective art educator, she must expose her students to a variety of materials and inspire them to approach these materials without preconceptions.

Fuller applied her progressive, Bauhaus-inspired approach in her classroom at MoMA, where she taught design to high school students. The results of her class's efforts came in early 1947, when the museum mounted *Experiments in Mobile Design* in its Young People's Gallery. According to the press release and installation photos, the show featured 'constructions in wire, wood, glass, colour transparencies', including several 'colour organs', which involved 'the projection of changing designs on flat and three-dimensional screens' and, in two cases, synchronised music.[14] In her 1948 Guggenheim application, Fuller included an entire section on her 'contributions to creative education', highlighting the achievements of her students and how her pedagogical approach enabled them to see 'possibilities where before they had seen limitations'.[15] Her aim, she wrote, 'was to have them find out for themselves that the materials of an artist are not confined to what has been used before in the field of art; that any material can be transformed into aesthetic reality'.[16] Following Bauhaus principles of exploring novel properties of materials, Fuller emphasised that 'elements such as form, line, colour, cannot be considered singly ... but are so interrelated that they must be felt and used simultaneously in full; that frequently the material we are using has unexplored qualities above and beyond what we see on the surface'.[17]

Fuller was incredibly proud of *Experiments in Mobile Design* and considered it an achievement on a par with her own artwork. In fact, she

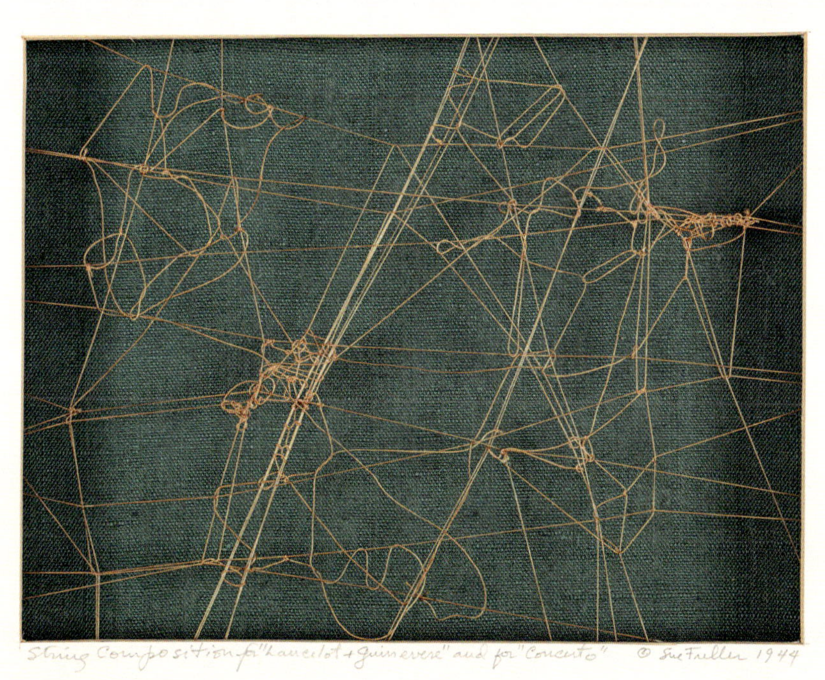

Fig.15
Sue Fuller, *String Composition for Lancelot and Guinevere and Concerto*, 1944
Matrix of stretched string and cord
12⅜ × 14⅜ × 1 in. (31.4 × 36.5 × 2.5 cm)
Museum of Fine Arts, Boston

contacted Henry Allen Moe, who headed the Guggenheim Foundation's grant programme, in advance of applying for a fellowship and invited him to see both *Mobile Design* and her first solo exhibition at the Village Art Center, which featured her Atelier 17 prints and was on view at the same time.[18] She encouraged active participation for visitors to *Mobile Design*, as was often suggested for full appreciation of Bauhaus objects. To Josephine Leighton, Moe's assistant, who saw both of Fuller's shows, the artist instructed: 'Some of the exhibits are mechanical be sure to push all the buttons & look in all the peep shows!'[19] Fuller's friend the photographer Eileen Darby even took portrait shots of Fuller posing within the wooden ladder structure on which her students' works were exhibited, and one of these photos is a composite with student work appearing along the margins (fig.13).

Fuller's professional colleagues recognised her enormous intellectual curiosity and commitment to gaining competency of specialised crafts and exploring the aesthetic potential of everyday materials. By the time she applied for the Guggenheim Fellowship, her record of innovating in the graphic arts was well established through her association with Atelier 17 and the resulting body of prints she made. Besides her extended experiments in transferring textures with soft-ground etching, she was also known at Atelier 17 for reconstituting a method for lift-ground etching, previously a trade secret. Adelyn Breeskin, then director of the Baltimore Museum of Art and formerly its curator of prints, wrote Fuller an enthusiastic recommendation for the fellowship. She stressed Fuller's technical command of the graphic arts and her forward-thinking outlook: 'She is the person best able to advance the scope of the graphic arts as an expression of our time ... Her enthusiasm is stimulating and inspiring. Her mind is awake to all phases of past accomplishments and future possibilities.'[20]

In his own letter of support, D'Amico stressed Fuller's eagerness to make interventions beyond the graphic arts and apply her Bauhaus-inspired approach to her own creative endeavours. He perfectly situates Fuller's inquisitive mind as rooted in the combination of a scientist's approach to research with the 'creative power of the artist'. His extended words are worth quoting in full: 'She seeks to cut down the barriers between the arts and to show how such a medium as light, or such a material as glass can be used freely and creatively by the artist. Her process breaks down the barriers between the arts and liberates the artist so that he confronts his subject, his ideas, and material, as an explorer.'[21] That last word, 'explorer', seems the most apt for describing Fuller's insatiable curiosity and her infectious zeal for knowledge, both intellectual (scientific and historical study) and physical (craft-based and artisanal proficiency).

Although Fuller discussed her motivations for making string compositions, she was adamant that these works be open to the interpretations of individual viewers. Her 1948 Guggenheim application rehearses thoughts that she would formalise and expand in the article she penned for *Craft Horizons* in 1954 about the string compositions. In her plan for work, she states her desire to evoke 'the symbols of our culture today', which she identifies as 'radar, atomic research, aeronautics'. Rather than represent these symbols literally, she insists the artist must generate 'a new form of expression – a new poetry of infinity'. Spurred by concepts of twentieth-century engineering – 'balance, motion, suspension, tension' – Fuller further clarifies how she intends to reach for this 'new poetry of infinity' with her ongoing work with glass and line. 'To me,' she writes, 'light and transparency convey the feeling of limitlessness which is becoming more and more apparent in every field of human endeavour.'[22]

Adding to the concepts of engineering, Fuller subsequently layered additional sources of inspiration based on her wide-ranging and near constant consumption of information. These inputs included study of lace, through books and consultation with lace experts, and reading about the role of string in storytelling and gameplay in non-Western cultures, namely through Kathleen Haddon's book *Artists in String: String Figures, their Regional Distribution and Social Significance* (1930).[23] Music was another metaphor she developed, in an article for the *Christian Science Monitor* in 1965: 'It is not by chance that these works are called String Compositions – a term usually associated with music ... I design the frames: they are the instruments. The passage of overlapping threads are to me a symphony of visual harmonies which are ordered by the intervals of the instrument. The composition may be simple or complex in an infinity of variation.'[24] Certainly, music and sound were a theme in her printmaking, with titles such as *Concerto* (1944), *Cacophony* (1944, pp.36–37) and even *New York, New York!* (1950, p.39), perhaps a reference to the song in the 1944 musical *On the Town*. In striving for the concept of limitlessness – her so-called 'new poetry of infinity' – Fuller intended her string compositions to have universal appeal. In the same piece for the *Christian Science Monitor*, she claims the string compositions are multifaceted and open-ended: 'I don't insist anybody see in them what I see. One person sees certain things, and somebody else sees other things.'[25] For this reason, she refrained from giving the pieces specific titles, only numbering them.

Whether inspiring viewers with her string compositions or coaching her students to find meaning through their own constructions, Fuller strove towards a utopian goal of leaving the world more unified and tolerant. She spelled out this view clearly in multiple published writings. In a 1943 article for *Design*, she emphasised the necessity of maintaining art education even during wartime, because it provided children a positive outlet to process current events. Furthermore, she feared, 'To leave the next generation without experience in the constructive elements of art which are ever at work over and above the barriers of nationality, language, and politics, is to leave them without understanding of the harmony of living.' Believing her role as an art teacher was tantamount to 'fighting ... for the rights of fundamental Freedom for all mankind', she argued her students might 'grasp the basic fundamentals of life's integration, the feeling for order and cooperation so necessary to the realization of a better world'.[26] As her career progressed, she continued to advocate for the power of art to bring people of the world together. Describing her inquiry into the history and cultural significance of strings in *Craft Horizons*, she ultimately concluded: 'the most important part [of this research] ... lies in the realization that art has always belonged to all people at all times and includes all mediums'.[27] Fuller lived these truths in her interactions with others – she was a generous colleague, teacher and collaborator, extending her support and sharing her expertise even in instances where there were language barriers.[28]

Despite the clarity of her motivations, Fuller struggled to find receptive audiences and mid-century critics who would embrace her vision of the string compositions and their Bauhaus-inspired purpose. After presenting the first group of string compositions as 'collages' in their debut at Bertha Schaefer Gallery, Fuller adapted and attempted to define the works as either paintings or sculptures. As initially envisioned and executed, the string compositions were glazed on both sides so they were transparent and viewable from front or back – as demonstrated in the full-page spread of Fuller in *Life* magazine from 1949 (fig.1, p.6) and in a late, site-specific commission for the McNay Art Museum in San Antonio, Texas (fig.16). This vision, which forced active viewer participation, came with its trade-offs. Critics often reviewed the string compositions as 'decorative' objects, a pejorative term that demoted them in the hierarchy of mid-century arts to the realm of craft.[29] Additionally, Fuller encountered institutional inflexibility to installing the string compositions as she intended: off the walls. She recounted one instance of a group show at the Whitney Museum of American Art where its curators mandated all work must sit flat against a wall and refused her an exception.[30] Eventually, Fuller decided to affix coloured backings to the works and submit them as 'paintings', which seemed to work acceptably within the art world structures of the time. One critic praised her as 'a painter in strings', and works like *String Composition #11* (1946, p.38) found entry into important exhibitions, such as Andrew Carnduff Ritchie's *Abstract Painting and Sculpture in America* (1951) at the Museum of Modern Art.[31] But this alliance was always tenuous.

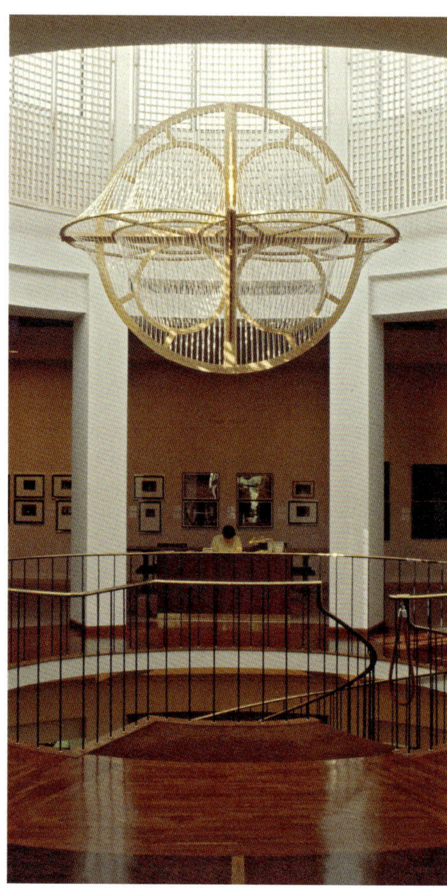

Fig.16
Sue Fuller, *String Composition #W-253*, 1984
Mahogany, brass and cord
144 × 168 × 168 in. (365.8 × 426.7 × 426.7 cm)
McNay Museum, San Antonio, Texas (Gift of Robert L. B. Tobin and the Friends of the McNay in honor of Margaret Batts Tobin)

In her lifetime, Fuller witnessed scholars attempt to shoehorn her string compositions into other creative movements of the twentieth century. For example, her *String Composition #119* (1964) was included in the Museum of Modern Art's notable Op art exhibition *The Responsive Eye* in 1965, a context that art historian Frances Follin recently unpacked and questioned.[32] In 1972, Mildred Constantine and Jack Lenor Larsen praised Fuller in their book *Beyond Craft: The Art Fabric* as a pioneer of what became known as fibre art.[33] Fuller was pleased to be named a pioneer of anything; but her string compositions have failed to gain traction within that subfield. Fuller also resisted association during the 1970s with feminist art, even as some activists cited her string compositions as some of the rare works by 'token' women artists represented in major museum collections.[34]

The present exhibition of Fuller's string compositions – the first major display since her death – presents a chance to view these works anew as the artist intended. They are not static objects to be regarded on the wall, but rather prisms bending light and line through space with limitless possibility. Their abstract, geometric forms connect with viewers regardless of language or nationality. Fuller would have loved the potential of seeing these twentieth-century objects through a twenty-first-century viewer's eyes. The string compositions will of course remain rooted in their time, and tied to their creator, but Fuller's 'new poetry of infinity' prescribed the string compositions' ongoing relevance – perhaps extending now to visualising the spread of pathogens, thinking about computer networks or mapping social and professional relationships.

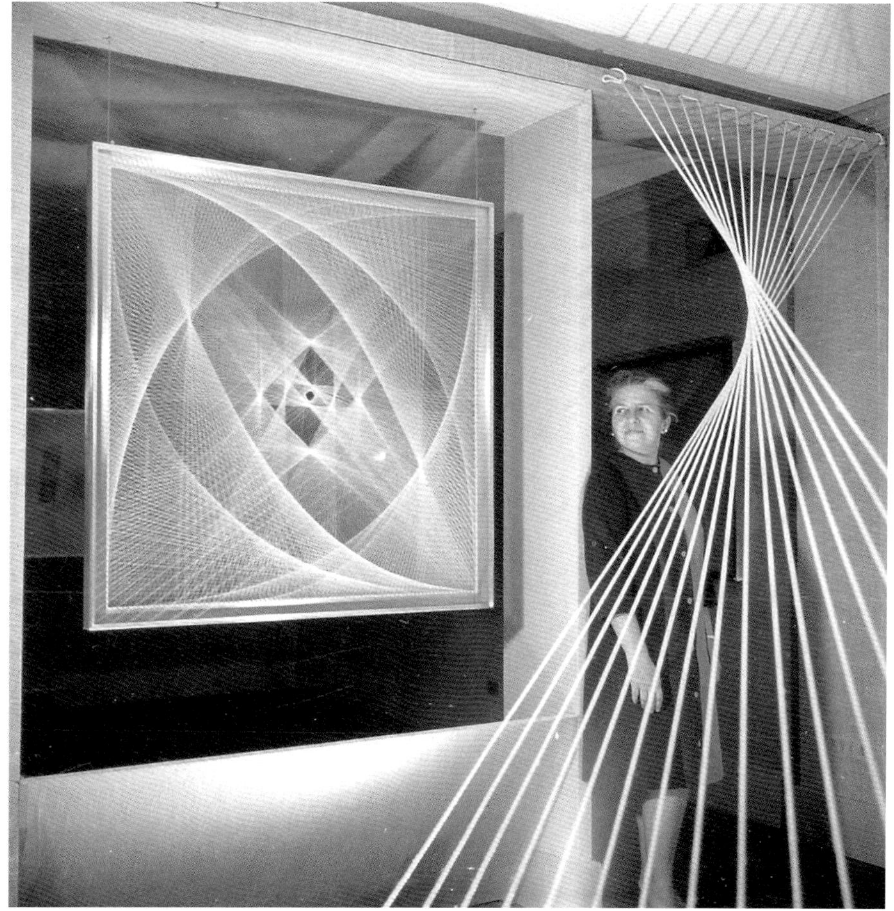

Fig.17
Installation view of *String Compositions, Plastic Embedments, Watercolors, Prints and Collages by Sue Fuller*, 28 June–28 August 1966, Storm King Art Center, New York

1 The press release for Fuller's 1949 show at Bertha Schaefer Gallery states: 'The first of the string compositions in this exhibition was made in 1946.' The Frick Art Reference Library, New York, has a copy of the press release attached to the exhibition brochure: Press release, 'Casein Paintings by Peter Busa, String Compositions by Sue Fuller', Bertha Schaefer Gallery, New York, 28 March–16 April 1949.

2 For more about Atelier 17's history, see Joann Moser, *Atelier 17: A 50th Anniversary Retrospective Exhibition*, exhibition catalogue, Elvehjem Art Center, University of Wisconsin, Madison, WI, 1977; Christina Weyl, *The Women of Atelier 17: Modernist Printmaking in Midcentury New York*, Yale University Press, New Haven, CT and London, 2019.

3 Fuller summarises how she used her grant money in a letter to Josephine Leighton, 14 January 1950, John Simon Guggenheim Memorial Foundation, New York (hereafter JSGMF). For Fuller's article, see 'Mary Cassatt's Use of Soft-Ground Etching', *Magazine of Art*, February 1950, pp.54–57.

4 The Guggenheim Foundation's file on Fuller spans the years 1946 to 1986 – covering three applications in 1948 and renewal proposals for 1950 and 1963 – and provides a rare chance to observe Fuller's views about the string compositions emerge and evolve over time. Thank you to André Bernard, Vice President at JSGMF, for providing access to Fuller's application materials.

5 Among others, she consulted with Dr Robert Feller, Fellow at the Mellon Institute of Industrial Research in Pittsburgh, and with industry such as Rohm & Haas, American Cyanamid, Owens-Corning Fiberglas, Pittsburgh Plate Glass and Dow Chemical.

6 Jeffrey Saletnik, 'Pedagogic Objects: Josef Albers, Greenbergian Modernism, and the Bauhaus in America', in Jeffrey Saletnik and Robin Schuldenfrei (eds), *Bauhaus Construct: Fashioning Identity, Discourse and Modernism*, Routledge, London, 2009, pp.83–102. Salentik's book on the same subject, *Josef Albers, Late Modernism, and Pedagogic Form*, is forthcoming from University of Chicago Press (2022).

7 Press release, 'Peter Busa/Sue Fuller', Bertha Schaefer Gallery, *op. cit.*

8 For more information about the relationship between Fuller's prints and collage, see Christina Weyl, 'The Printed Collage', in Alex J. Taylor, Christina Weyl and Frances Follin, '*String Composition 128* (1964) by Sue Fuller', Tate Research Publication, 2018, www.tate.org.uk/research/in-focus/string-composition-128, accessed 3 August 2022; Weyl, *Women of Atelier 17*, *op. cit.*, ch.3.

9 Weyl, *Women of Atelier 17*, *op. cit.*, pp.108–14.

10 Sue Fuller, letter to Jacob Kainen, 12 October 1947, Special Exhibition File (hereafter SEF), National Museum of American History, Smithsonian Institution, Washington, DC (emphasis original). For more information about the Special Exhibition Program, see Helena E. Wright, 'A National Audience for Prints: The Smithsonian's Special Exhibition Program, 1923–48', in David Tatham (ed), *North American Prints, 1913–1947: An Examination at Century's End*, 1st ed., Syracuse University Press, Syracuse, NY, 2006.

11 Sue Fuller, letter to Miss McLucas or Mrs Daugherty, 4 March 1963, JSGMF.

12 Fuller received a bachelor's degree in Fine Art from the Carnegie Institute of Technology, Pittsburgh (1936), took summer study with Ernest Thurn and Hans Hofmann in Gloucester, Massachusetts (1931 and 1934), and received a master's in Fine Arts from Teachers College, Columbia University, New York (1939).

13 Sue Fuller, oral history interview by Paul Cummings, 8 May 1975, Archives of American Art, Smithsonian Institution, Washington, DC. In her 1948 application to the Guggenheim Foundation, Fuller lists MoMA as her employer between 1944 and 1947. Information about the Bauhaus was somewhat slow to trickle into America until the mid-1930s. Margret Kentgens-Craig, *The Bauhaus and America: First Contacts, 1919–1936*, MIT Press, Cambridge, MA, 2001, p.105. In 1938, MoMA held a much discussed and debated exhibition about the Bauhaus. For further discussion, see Karen Koehler, 'The Bauhaus, 1919–1928: Gropius in Exile and the Museum of Modern Art, NY, 1938', in Richard Etlin (ed), *Art, Culture, and Media under the Third Reich*, University of Chicago Press, Chicago, 2002, pp.295–310.

14 Press release and installation photographs, *Experiments in Mobile Design* (14 January–13 April 1947), www.moma.org/calendar/exhibitions/3206, accessed 3 August 2022.

15 Sue Fuller, 'Nature of Teaching', Part I: Accomplishments, application to JSGMF, 1948, p.4.

16 *Ibid.*

17 *Ibid.*

18 Sue Fuller, letter to Henry Allen Moe, 21 February 1947, JSGMF. For the exhibition brochure for Fuller's first solo show, see 'First Prize Award Exhibition', 23 February–8 March 1947, SEF.

19 Sue Fuller to Josephine Leighton, 15 February 1947, JSGMF.

20 Adelyn Breeskin, recommendation letter for Sue Fuller, c.December 1947, JSGMF.

21 Victor D'Amico sent an unsolicited letter of recommendation to Henry Allen Moe, 3 February 1947, JSGMF. For more about D'Amico's pedagogy and his approach to the department of education at MoMA, see John R. Blakinger, 'MoMA's Child Artists: The Politics of Creating Creative Children', in Austin Porter and Sandra Salman (eds), *Modern in the Making: MoMA and the Modern Experiment, 1929–1949*, Bloomsbury Visual Arts, London, 2020, pp.49–64.

22 Sue Fuller, 'Ultimate Purpose', Part II: Plans for Work, application to JSGMF, 1948, p.6.

23 For more about Fuller's interest in string, see Alex J. Taylor, 'Common Threads', in Taylor, Weyl and Follin, *op. cit.*

24 Sue Fuller, 'Transparency, Light and Balance', *Christian Science Monitor*, 22 September 1965, p.8.

25 *Ibid.*

26 Sue Fuller, 'Shall We Scrap the Art Teacher in Time of War', *Design*, vol.44, no.5, January 1943, p.25.

27 Sue Fuller, 'Twentieth Century Cat's Cradle', *Craft Horizons*, vol.14, no.2, April 1954, p.24.

28 As a newly arrived Guggenheim Fellow from Argentina, Mauricio Lasansky spoke little English when he and Sue Fuller met at Atelier 17. Nevertheless, the two shared important technical tricks at the studio and maintained a lifelong friendship. Sue Fuller, oral history interview by Paul Cummings, 30 April 1975, Archives of American Art, Smithsonian Institution, Washington, DC.

29 See Alex J. Taylor's discussion of Fuller's work as 'decorative' in Alex J. Taylor, 'Introduction', in Taylor, Weyl and Follin, *op. cit.*

30 Fuller, oral history interview, 30 April 1975, *op. cit.*

31 This piece is alternatively titled *String Composition in Yellow and Grey*. Andrew Carnduff Ritchie, *Abstract Painting and Sculpture in America*, exhibition catalogue, Museum of Modern Art, New York, 1951, p.84.

32 Frances Follin, 'Unravelling Op', in Taylor, Weyl and Follin, *op. cit.*

33 Mildred Constantine and Jack Lenor Larson, *Beyond Craft: The Art Fabric*, Van Nostrand Reinhold, New York, 1972, pp.38, 40.

34 Sue Fuller, letter to Florence Forst, 4 May 1994, Sue Fuller letters to Florence Forst, 1950–1994, Archives of American Art, Smithsonian Institution, Washington, DC.

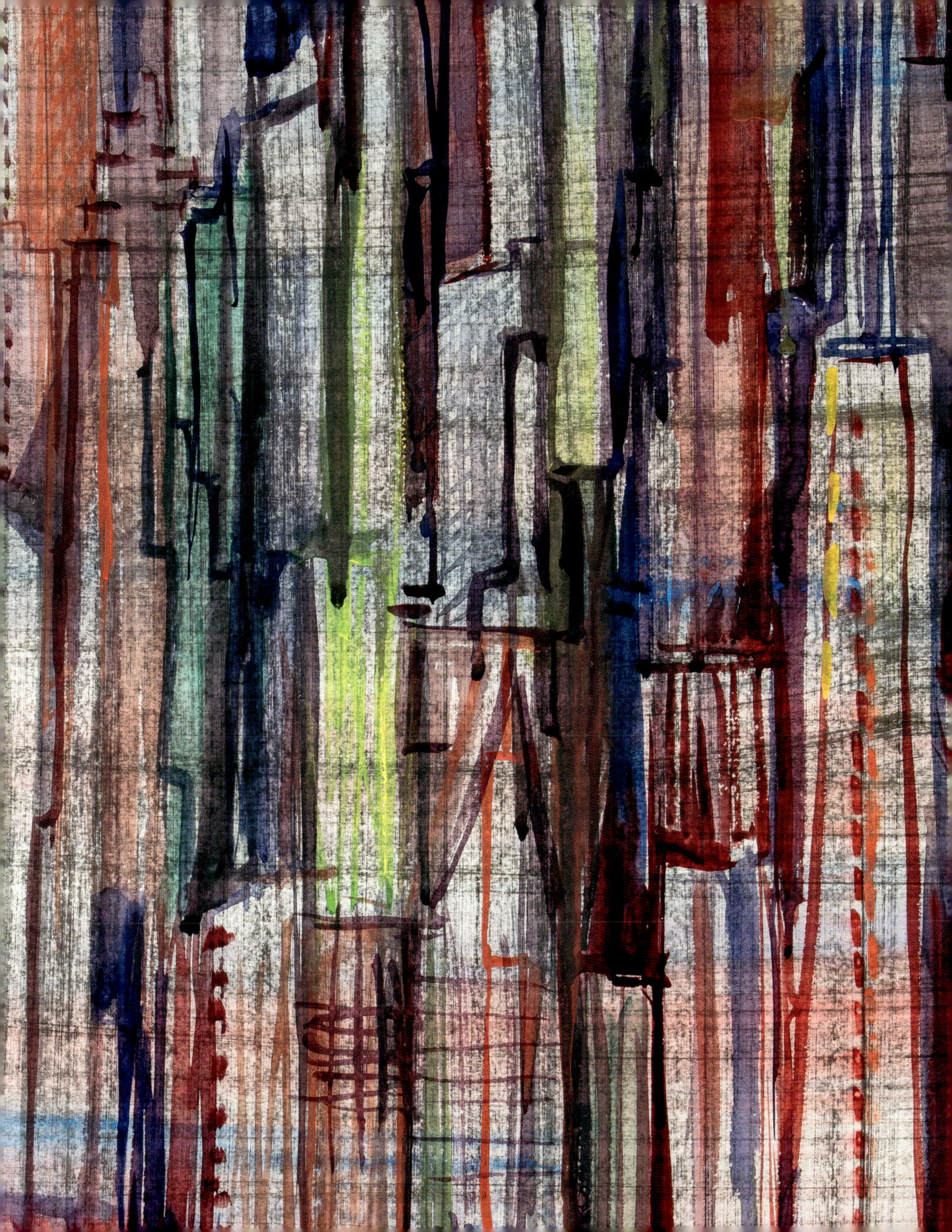

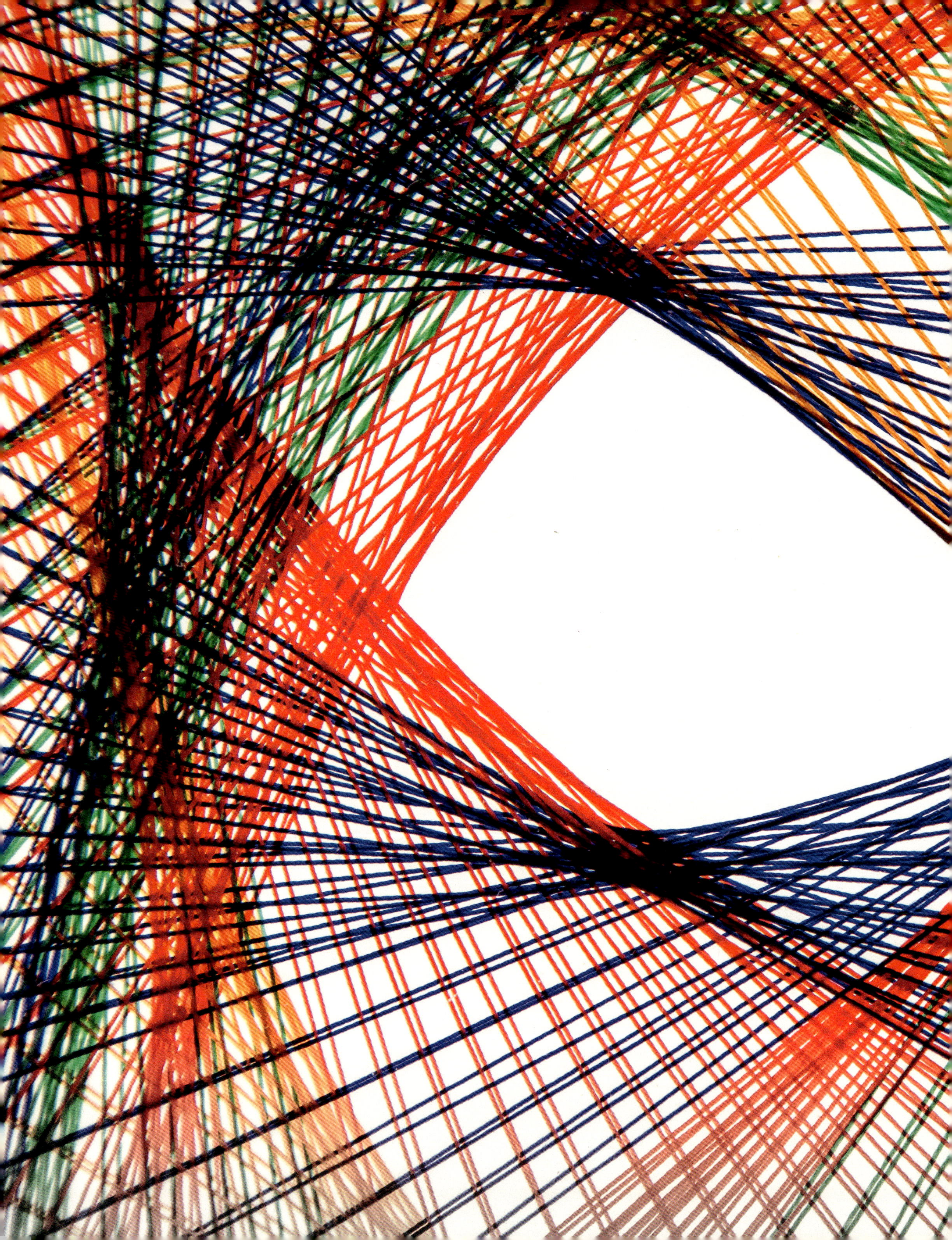

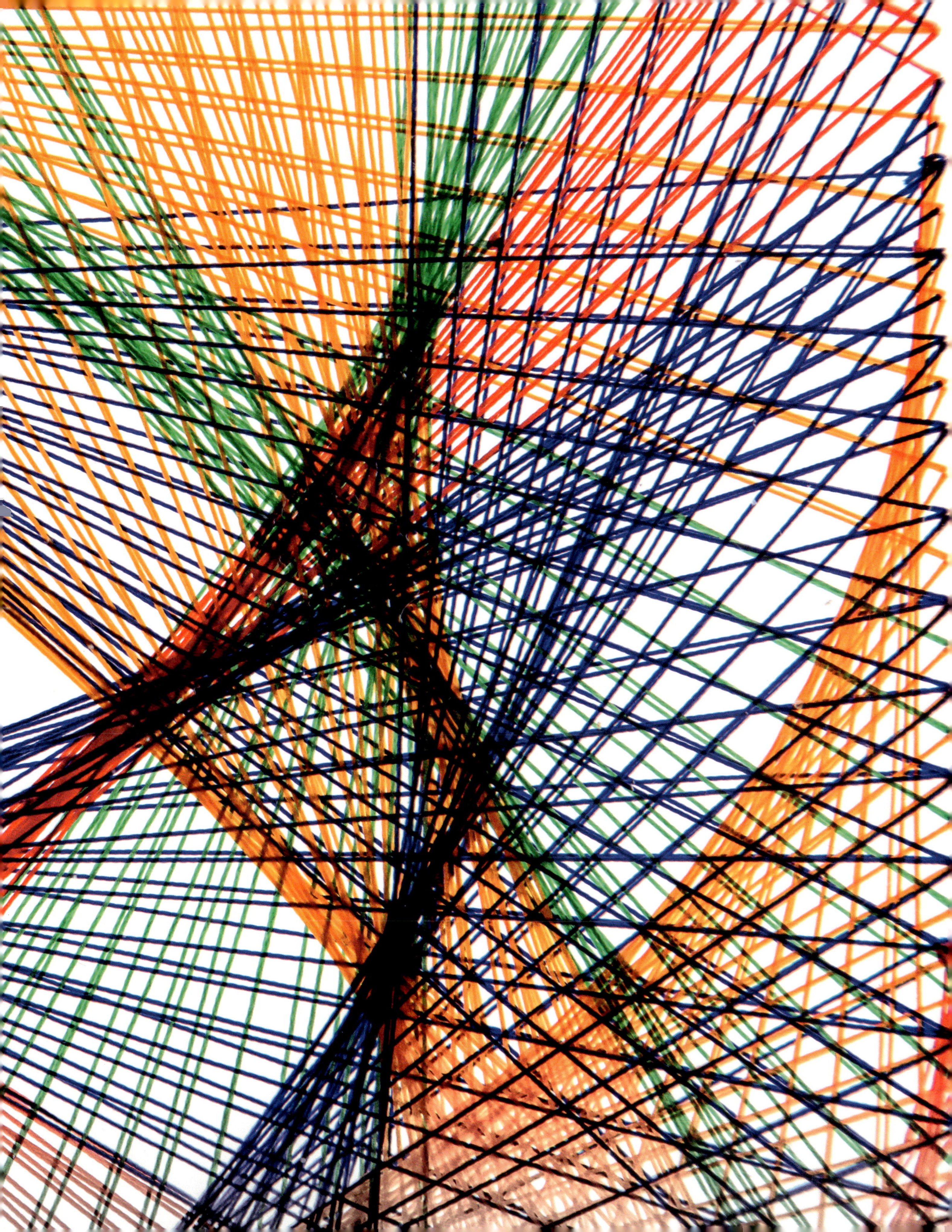

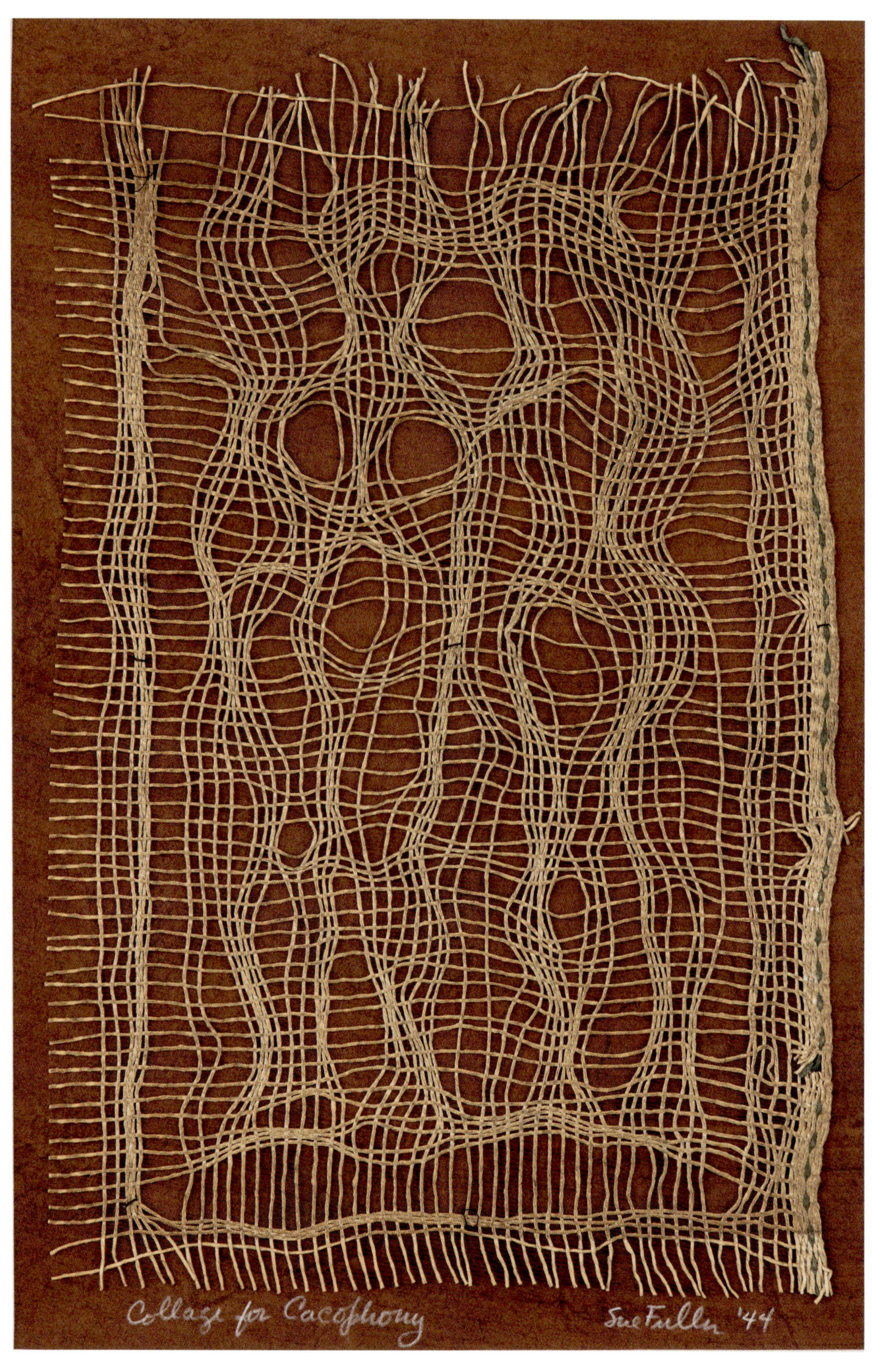

Sue Fuller, *Collage for Cacophony*, 1944
Thread on paper, 11 × 8 in. (28 × 20 cm)

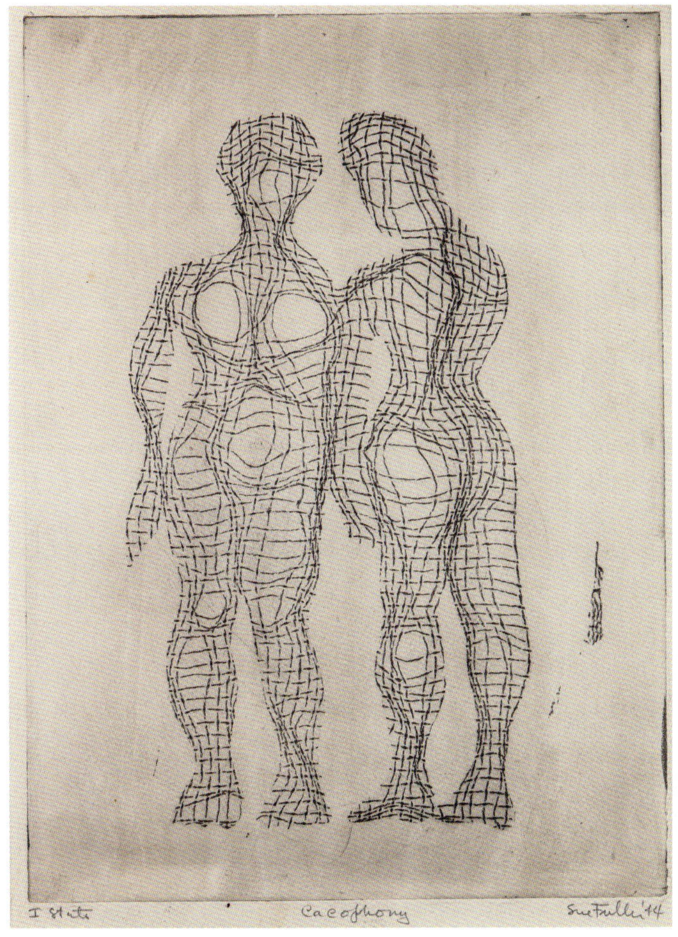

Sue Fuller, *Cacophony. First state*, 1944
Soft-ground etching, 12 × 8¾ in. (30.5 × 22 cm)

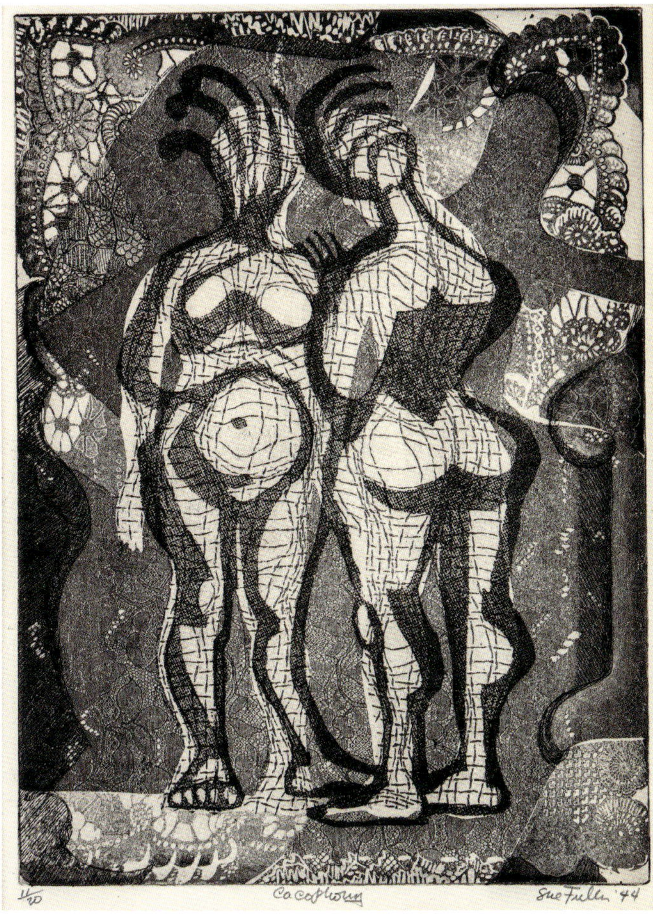

Sue Fuller, *Cacophony*, 1944
Soft-ground etching, 12 × 8¾ in. (30.5 × 22 cm)

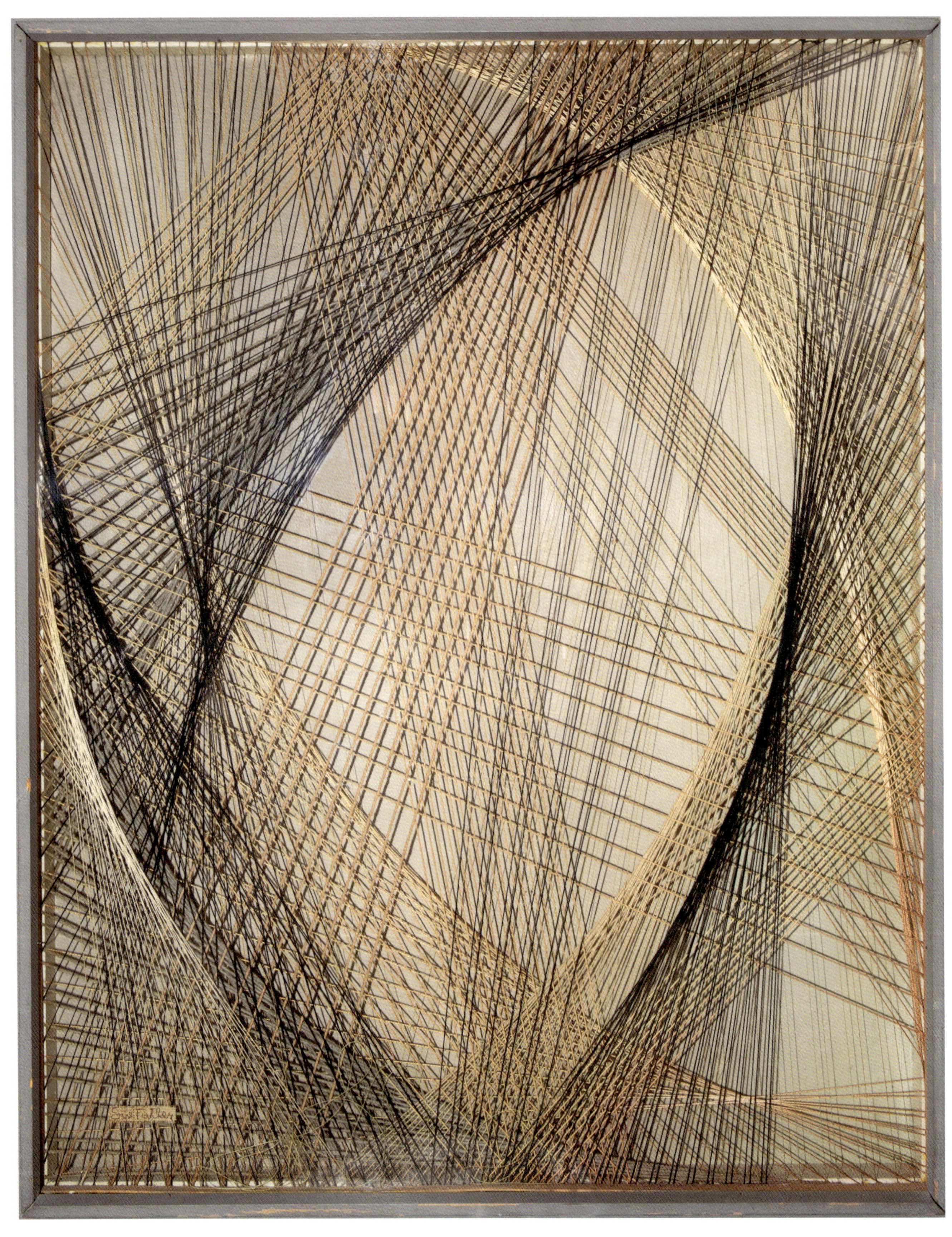

Sue Fuller, *String Composition #11*, 1946
String on wooden board, 32⅛ × 25¾ × 3 in. (81.5 × 65.5 × 7.5 cm)

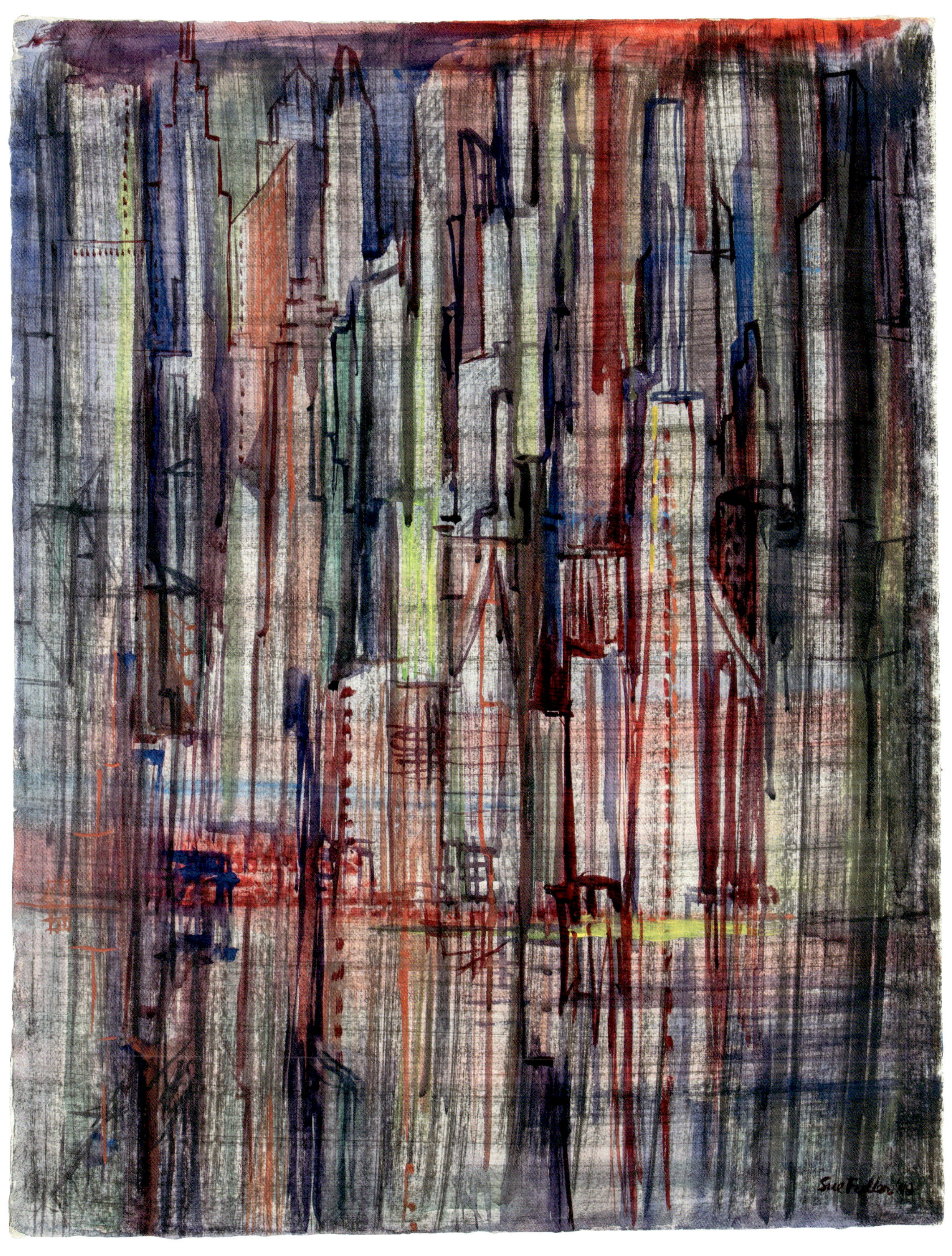

Sue Fuller, *New York, New York!*, 1949
Watercolour on paper, 20 × 15 in. (51 × 38 cm)

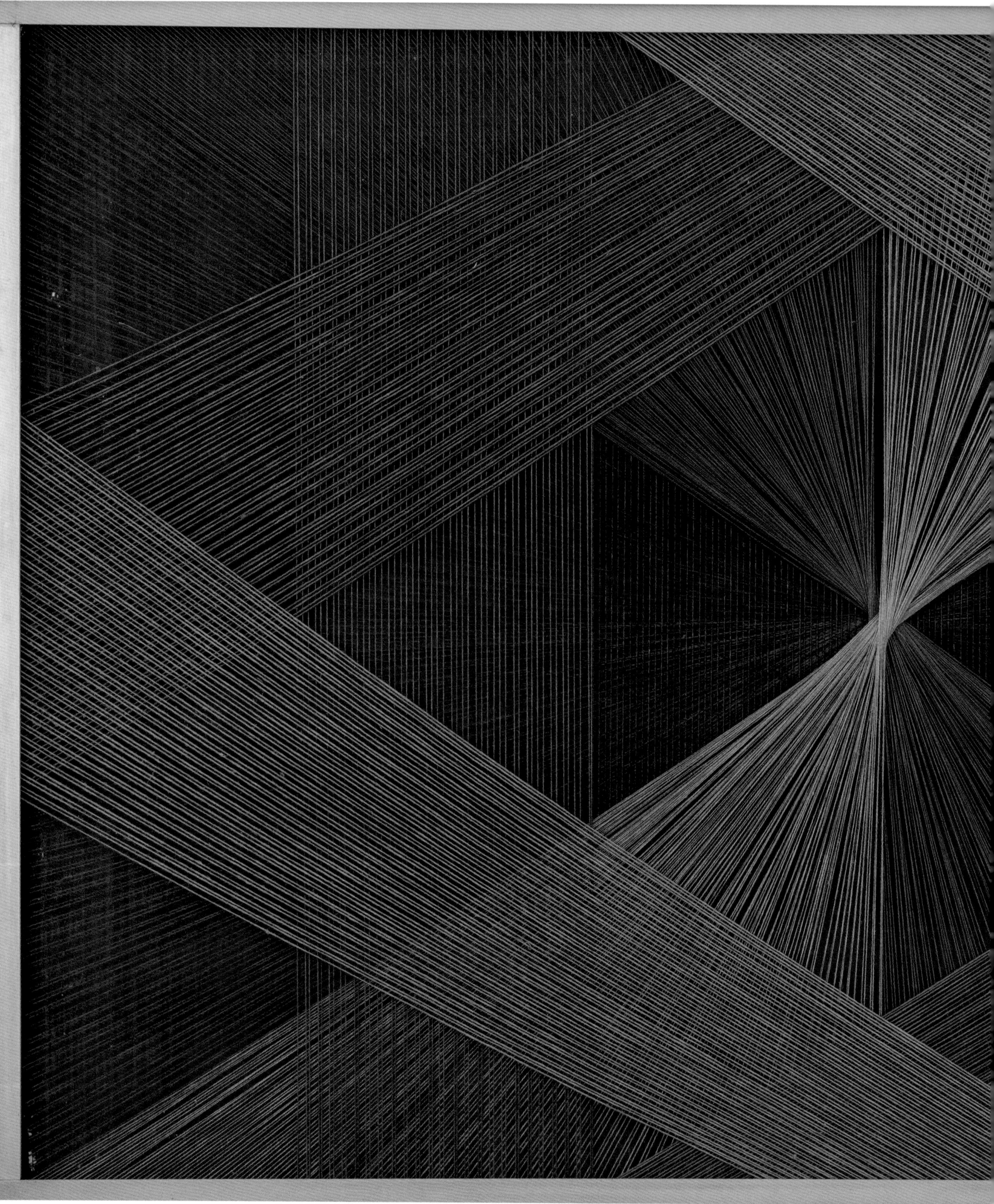

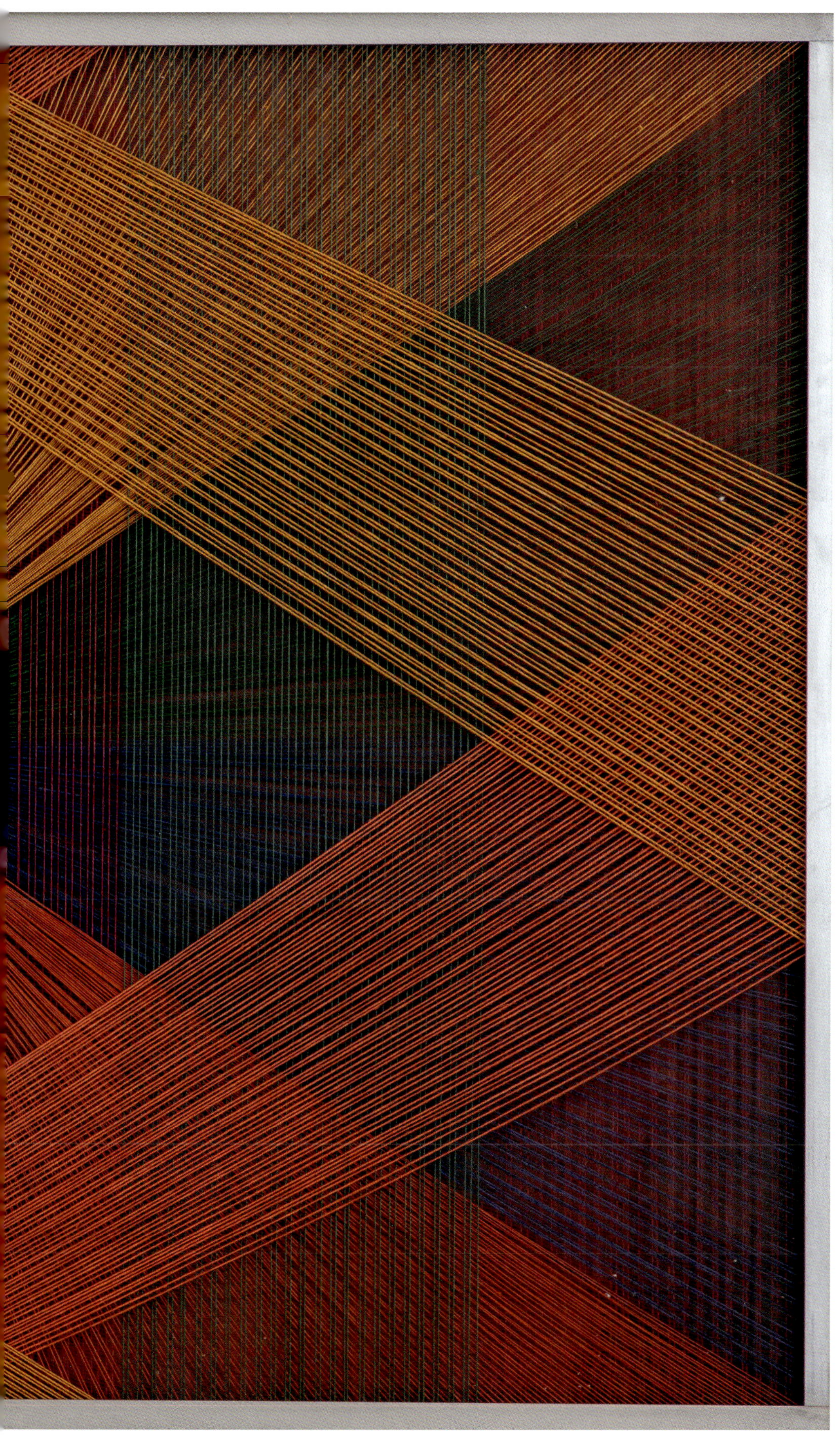

Sue Fuller, *Untitled*, c.1950s
Linen thread on canvas,
72½ × 48 × 2 in. (184 × 123 × 5.5 cm)

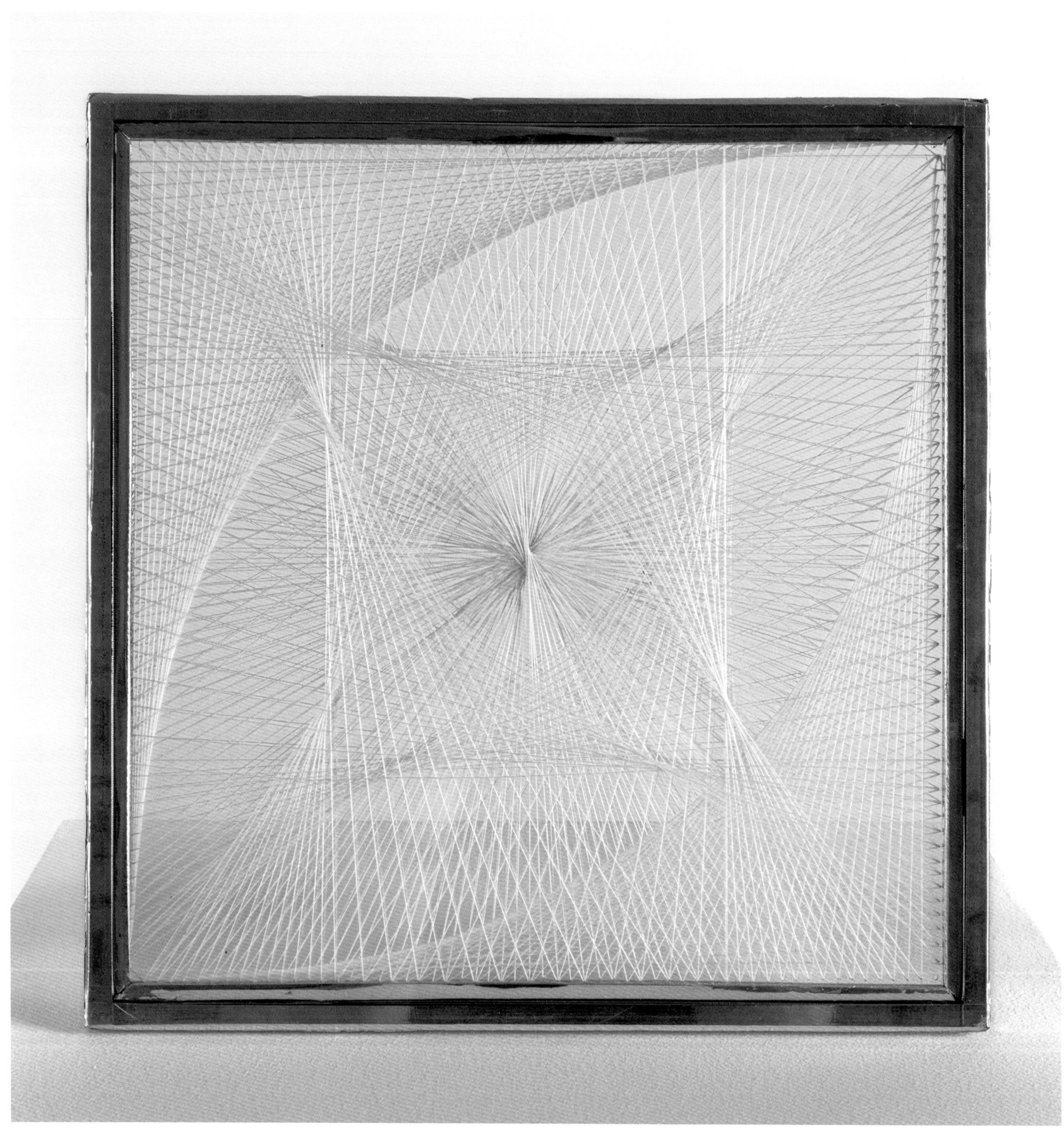

Sue Fuller, *Untitled*, c.1950s
White string and aluminium tape, 12 × 12 × ¾ in. (30.5 × 30.5 × 2 cm)

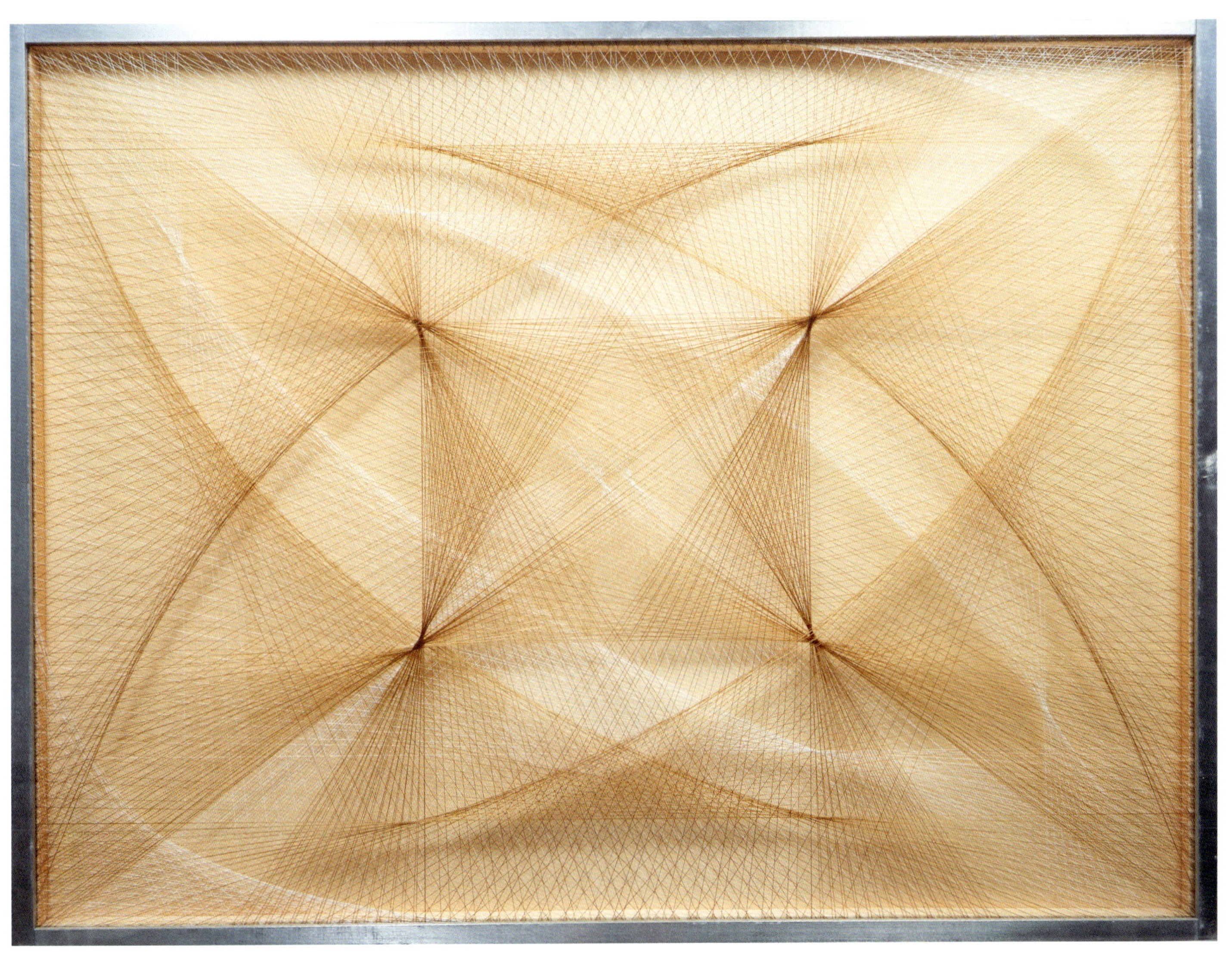

Sue Fuller, *String Composition #82*, 1957
String on silk, 48⅜ × 36⅝ in. (123 × 93 cm)

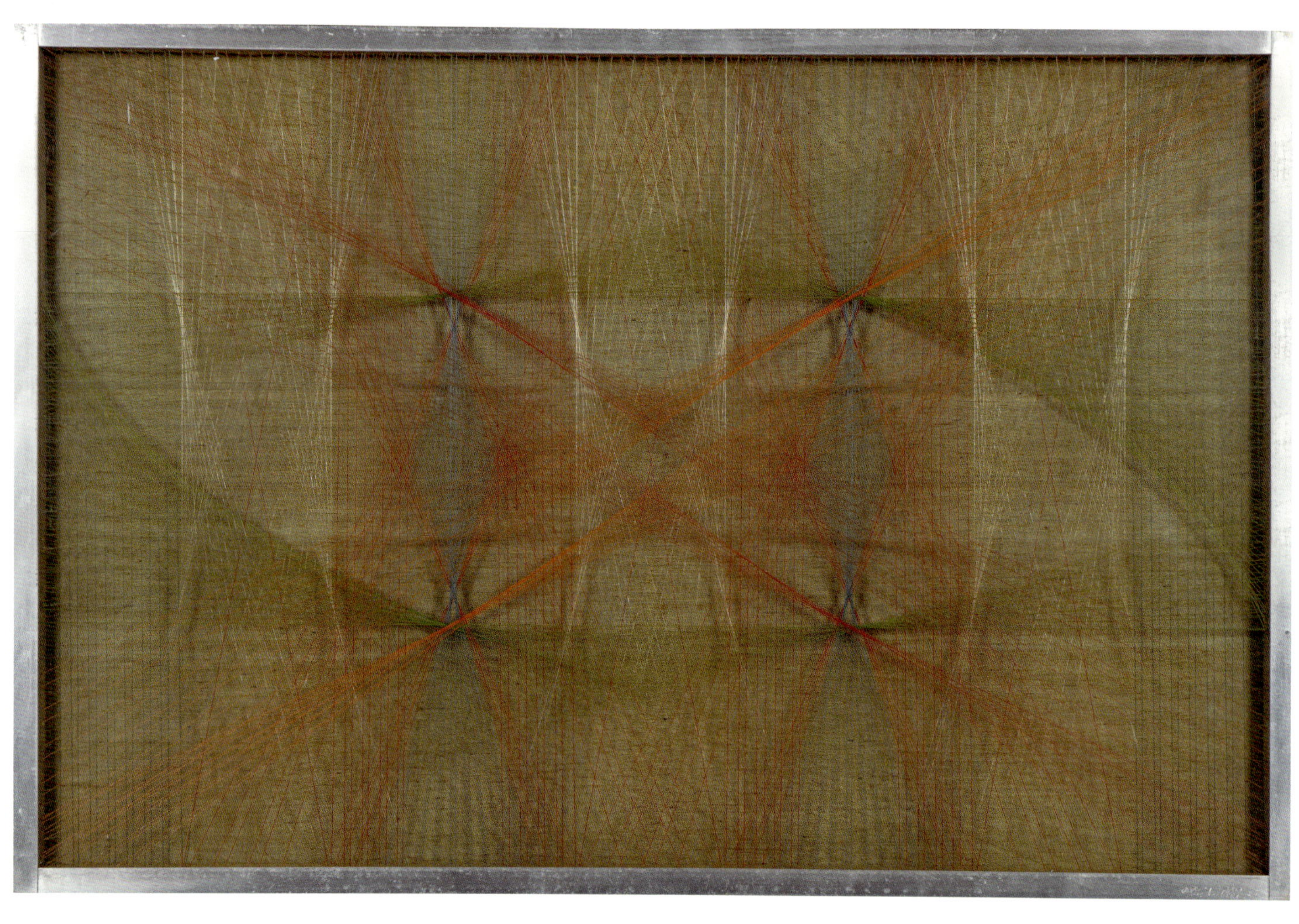

Sue Fuller, *String Composition #110*, 1961
Polypropylene thread and fabric laid on board,
24⅜ × 36⅜ × 1⅝ in. (62 × 92.5 × 4 cm)

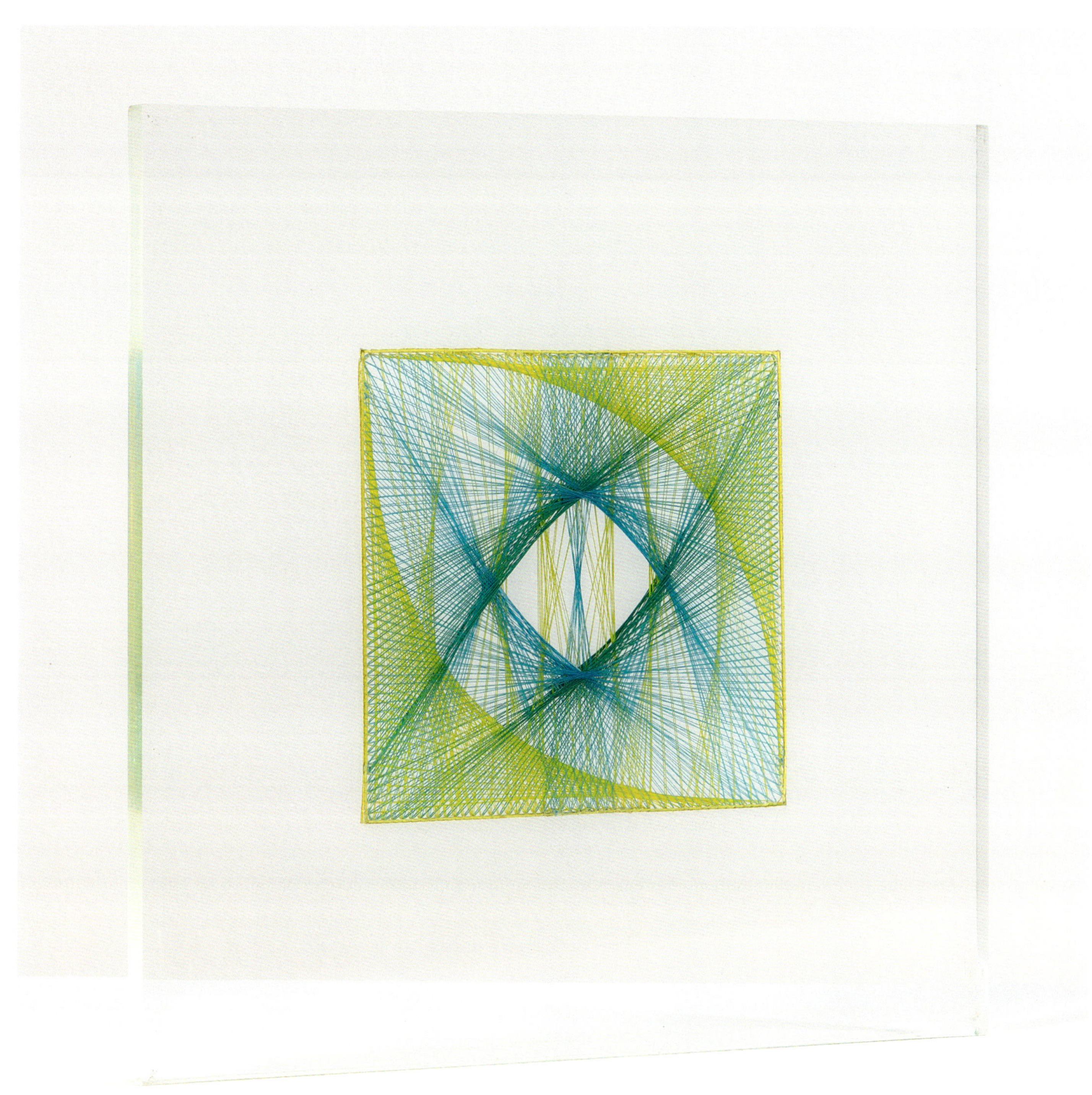

Sue Fuller, *String Composition #319*, 1964
Lucite and polypropylene thread, 11¾ × 11¾ × ⅝ in. (30 × 30 × 1.5 cm)

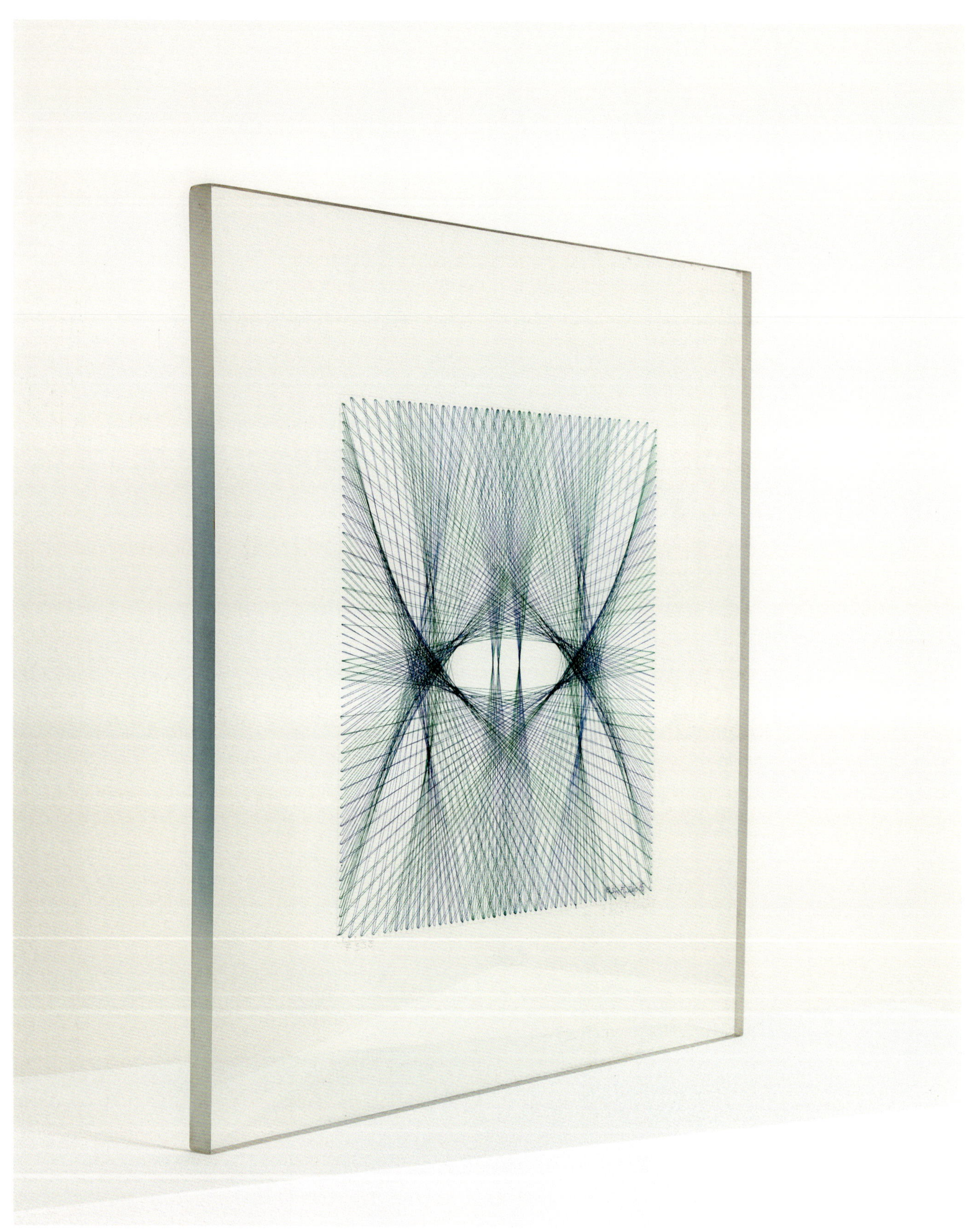

Sue Fuller, *String Composition #333*, 1965
Lucite and polypropylene thread, 25 × 25 × 1 in. (63.5 × 63.5 × 2.5 cm)

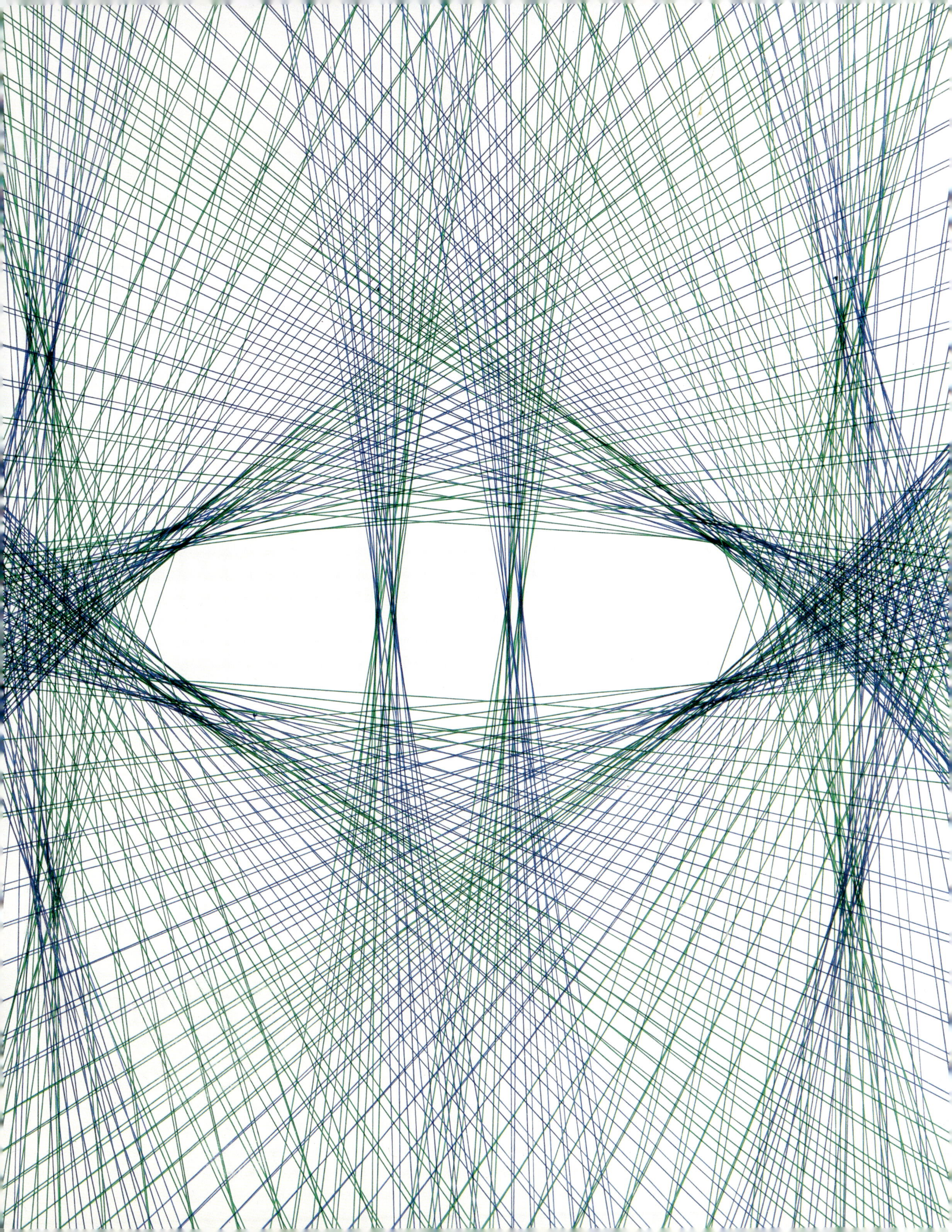

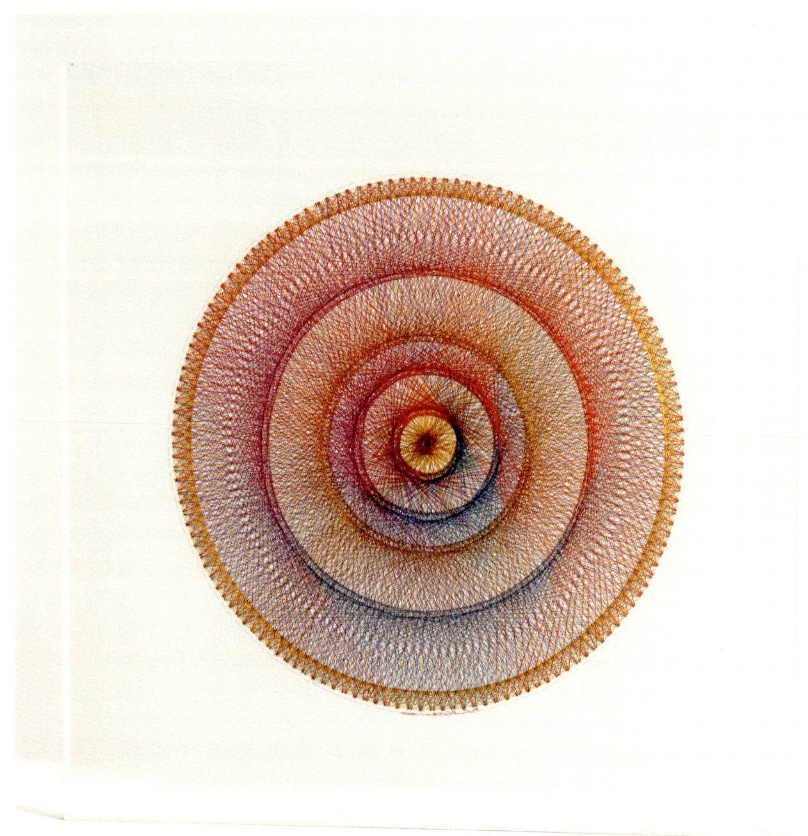

Sue Fuller, *String Composition #533*, 1966
Lucite and polypropylene thread,
21 × 21 × 1⅛ in. (53.5 × 53.5 × 3 cm)

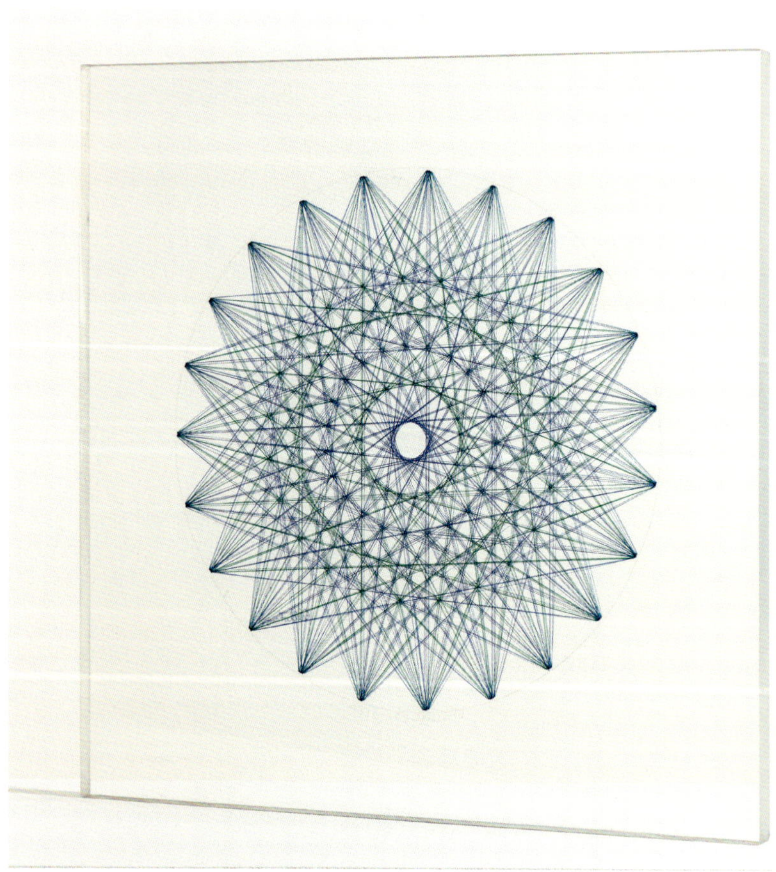

Sue Fuller, *String Composition #338*, 1964
Lucite and polypropylene thread,
21 × 21 × 1⅛ in. (53.5 × 53.5 × 3 cm)

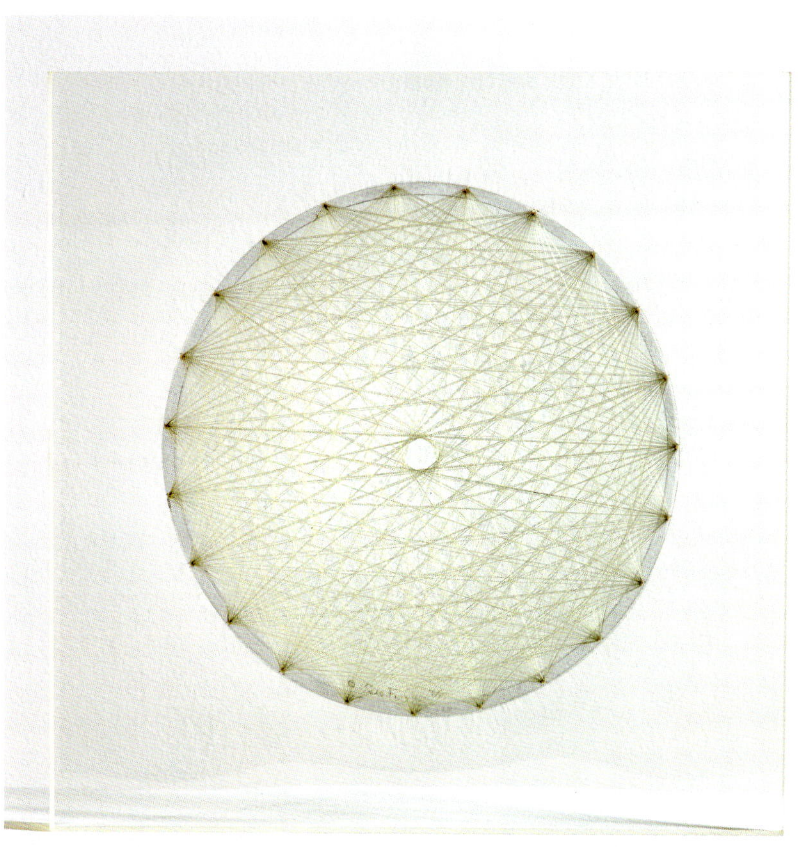

Sue Fuller, *String Composition #500*, 1965
Lucite and polypropylene thread,
17⅛ × 17⅛ × 1⅝ in. (43.5 × 43.5 × 4 cm)

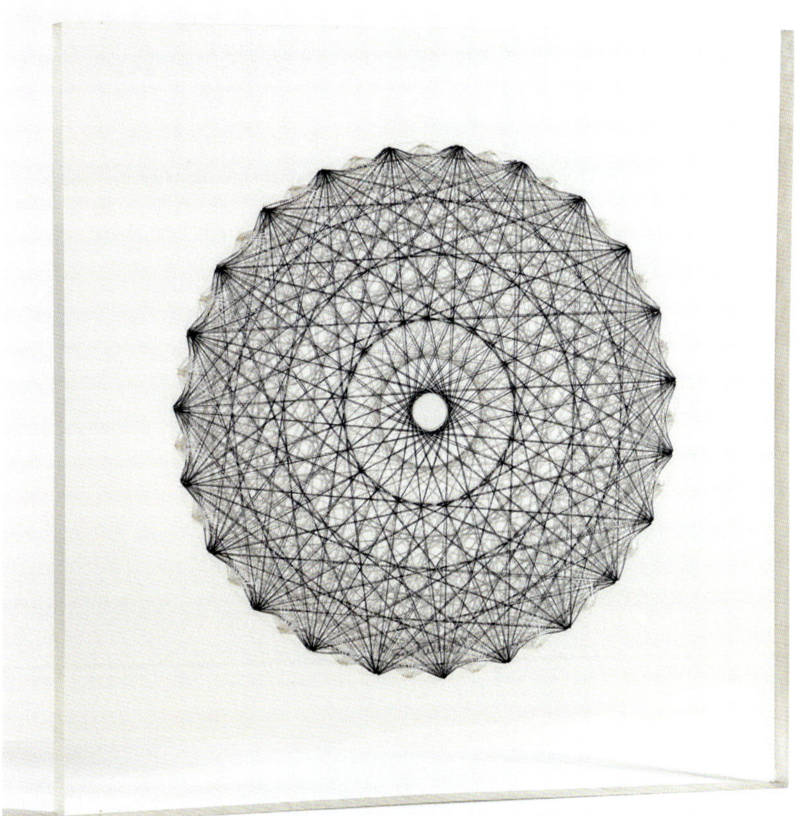

Sue Fuller, *String Composition #501*, 1965
Lucite and polypropylene thread,
17⅛ × 17⅛ × 1⅝ in. (43.5 × 43.5 × 4 cm)

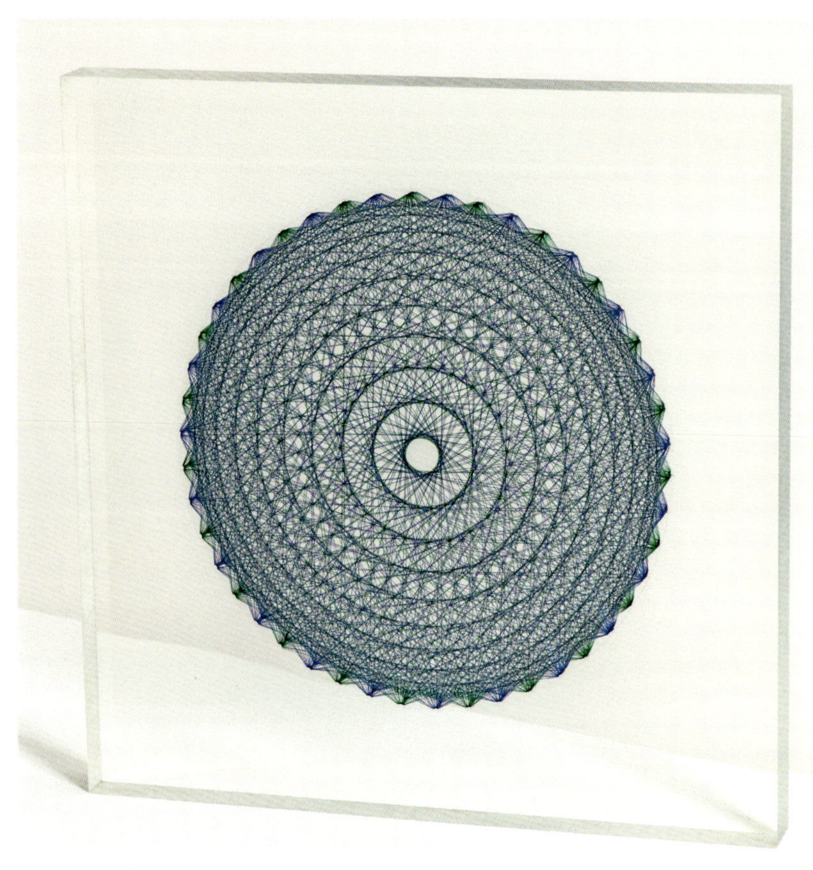

Sue Fuller, *String Composition #502*, 1965
Lucite and polypropylene thread,
16⅞ × 16⅞ × 1½ in. (43 × 43 × 3.5 cm)

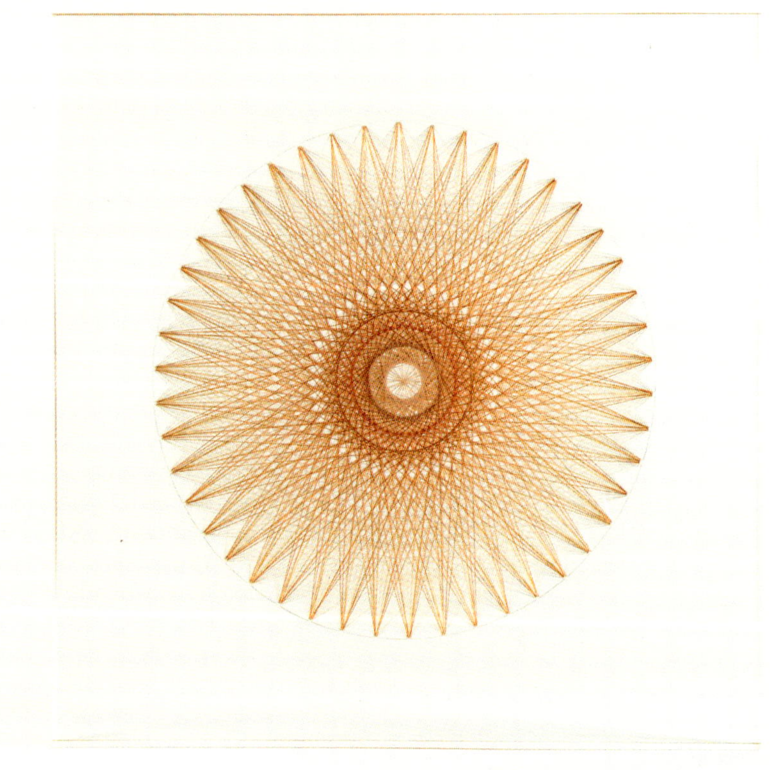

Sue Fuller, *String Composition #531*, 1965
Lucite and polypropylene thread,
21 × 21 × 1⅛ in. (53.5 × 53.5 × 3 cm)

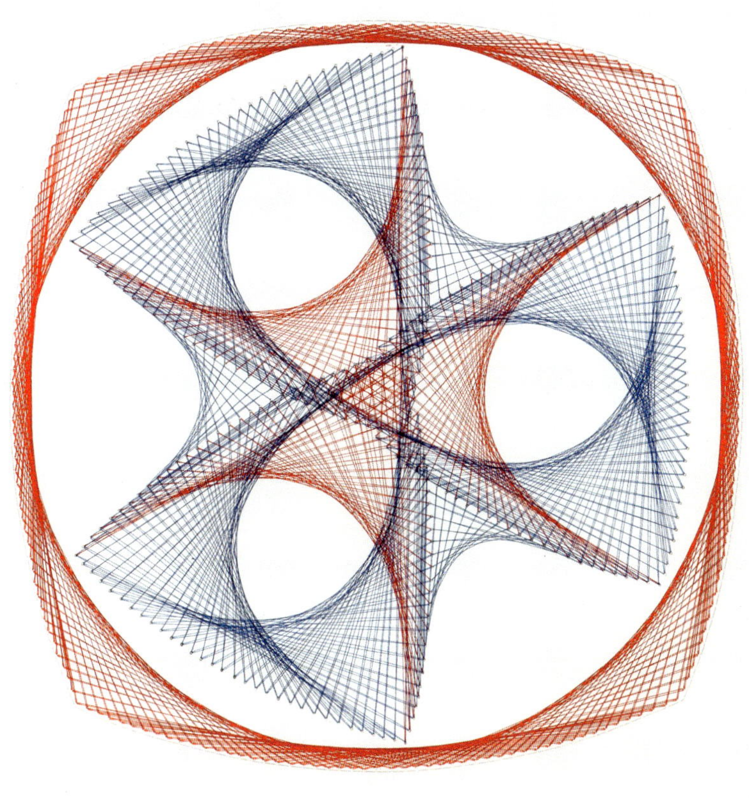

Sue Fuller, *String Composition #556*, 1968
Lucite and polypropylene thread, 25 × 25 × 1 in. (63.5 × 63.5 × 2.5 cm)

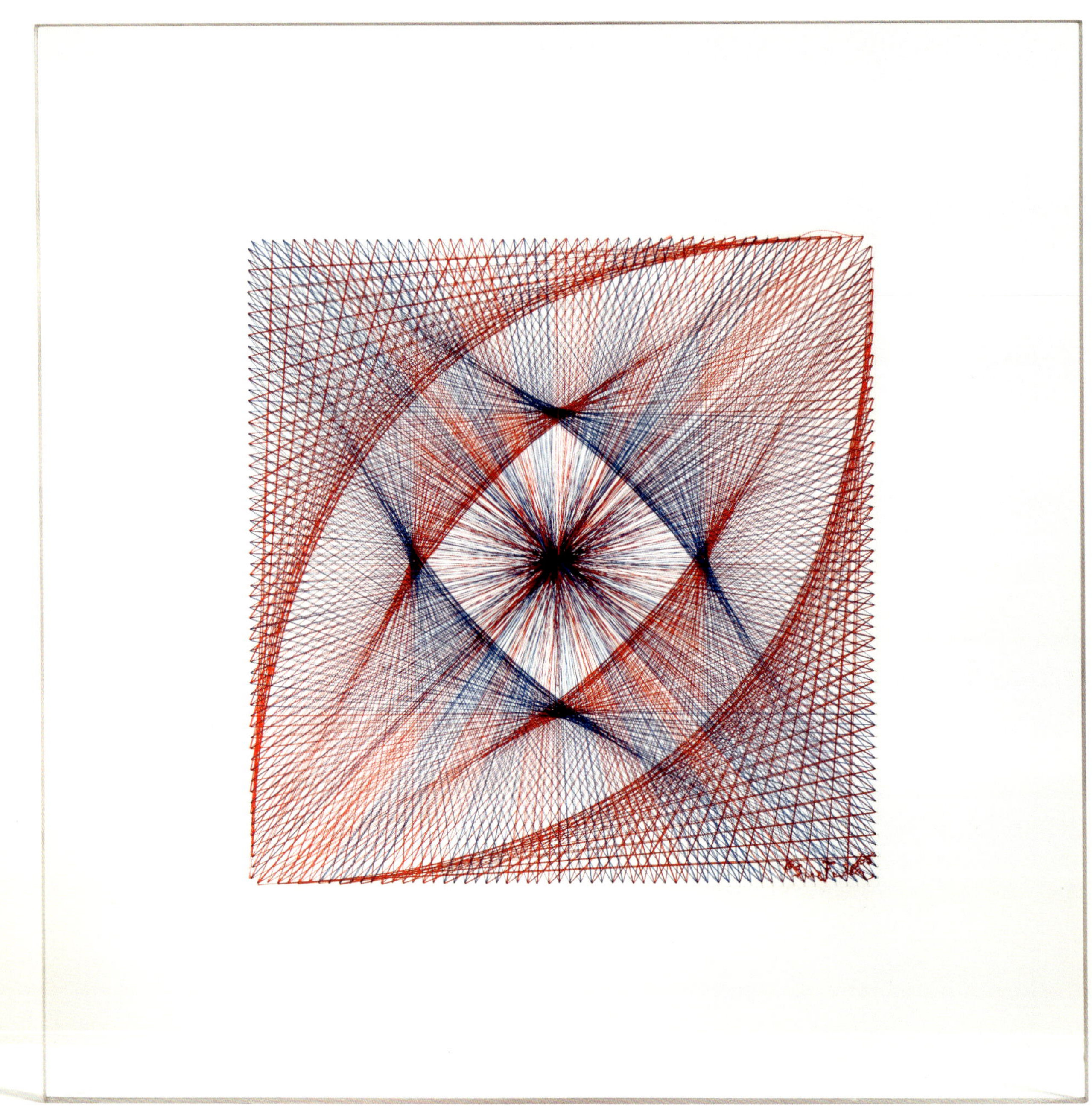

Sue Fuller, *String Composition #335*, 1965
Lucite and polypropylene thread, 25 × 25 × 1 in. (63.5 × 63.5 × 2.5 cm)

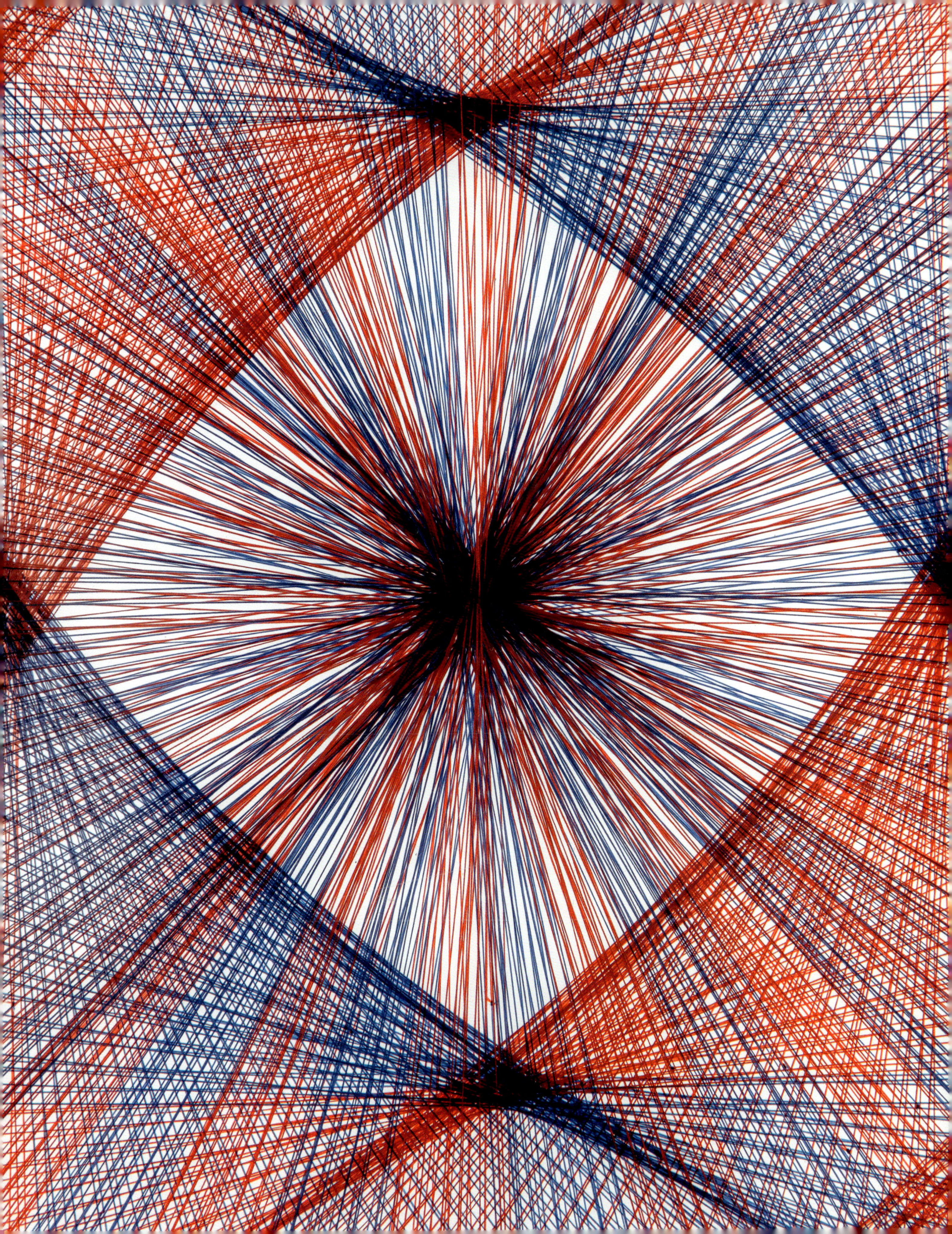

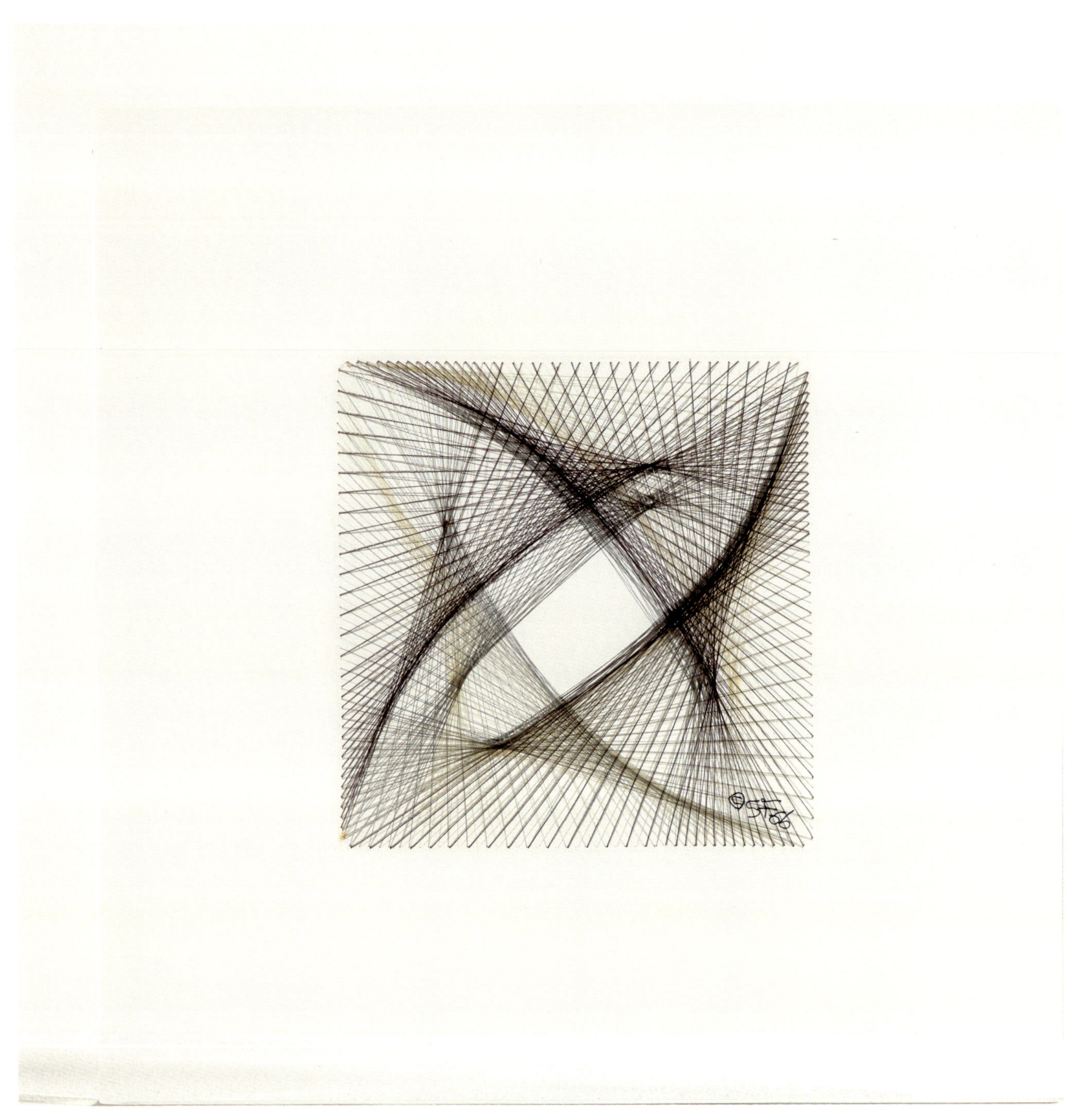

Sue Fuller, *String Composition #363*, 1966
Lucite and polypropylene thread, 12 × 12 × ¾ in. (30.5 × 30.5 × 2 cm)

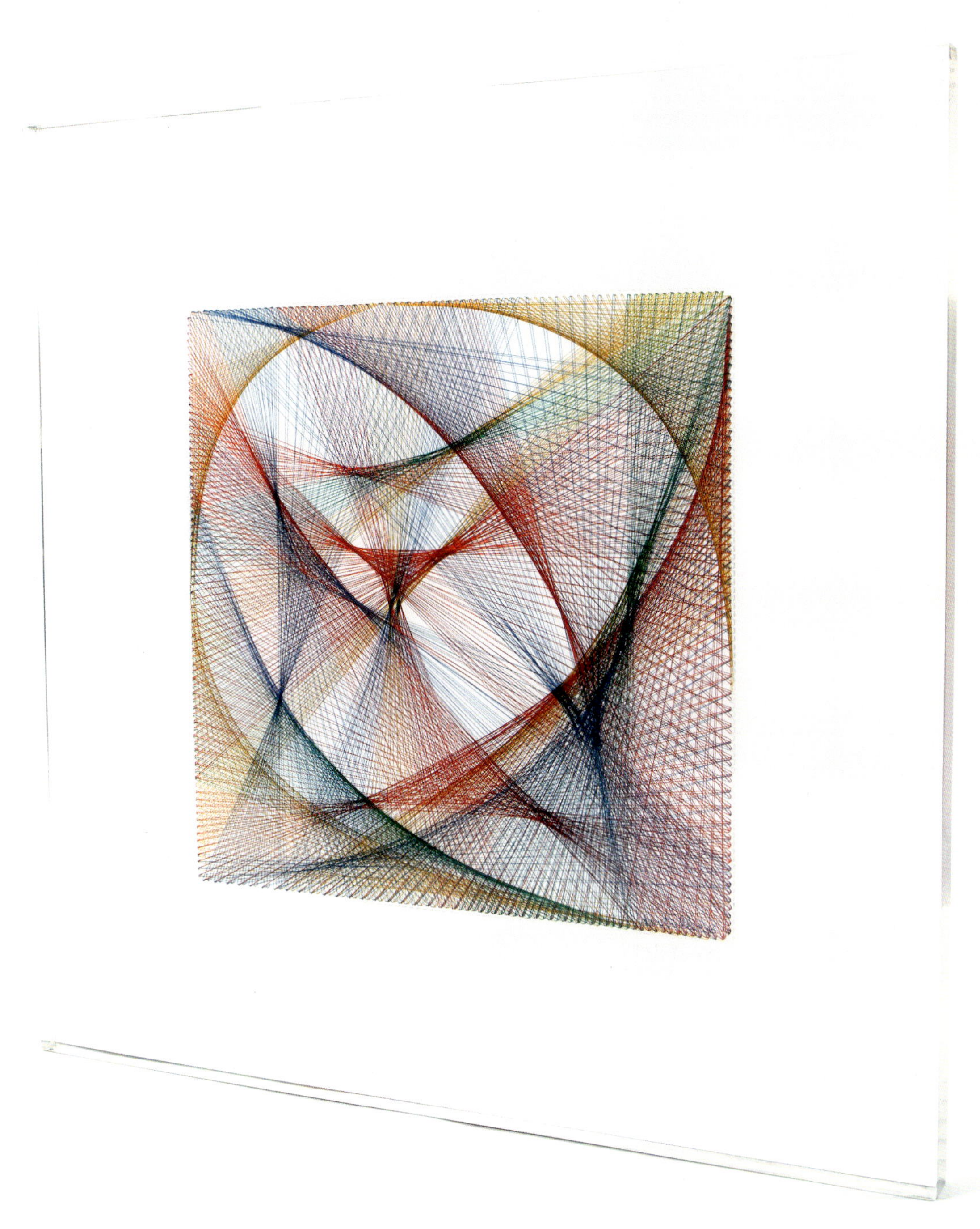

Sue Fuller, *String Composition #552*, 1966
Lucite and polypropylene thread, 25 × 25 × 1 in. (63.5 × 63.5 × 2.5 cm)

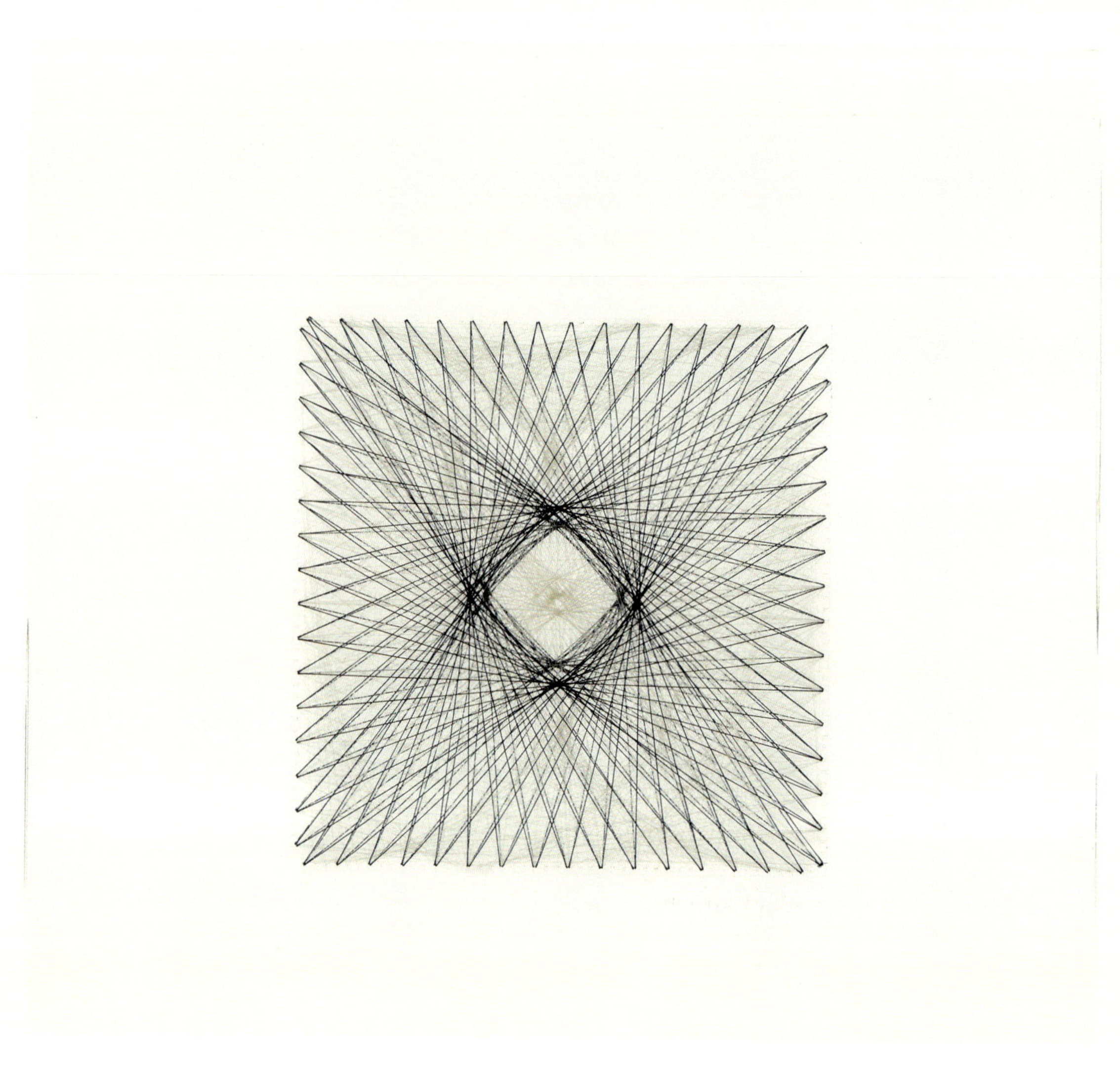

Sue Fuller, *String Composition #359*, 1965
Lucite and polypropylene thread, 12 × 12 × ¾ in. (30.5 × 30.5 × 2 cm)

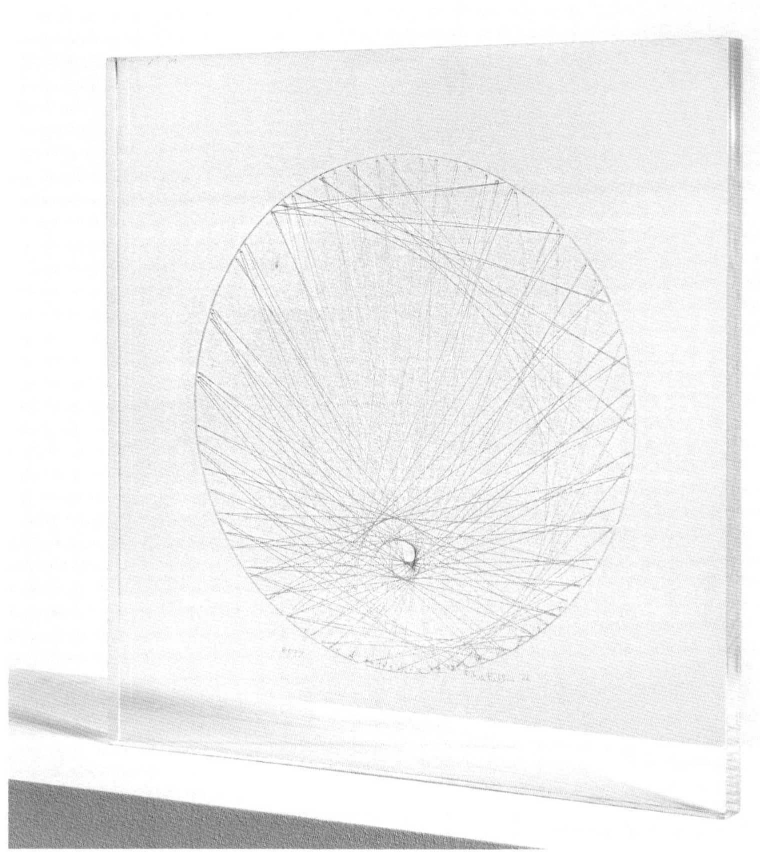

Sue Fuller, *String Composition #537*, 1966
Lucite and polypropylene thread,
21 × 21 × 1⅛ in. (53.5 × 53.5 × 3 cm)

Sue Fuller, *String Composition #535*, 1966
Lucite and polypropylene thread,
21 × 21 × 1⅛ in. (53.5 × 53.5 × 3 cm)

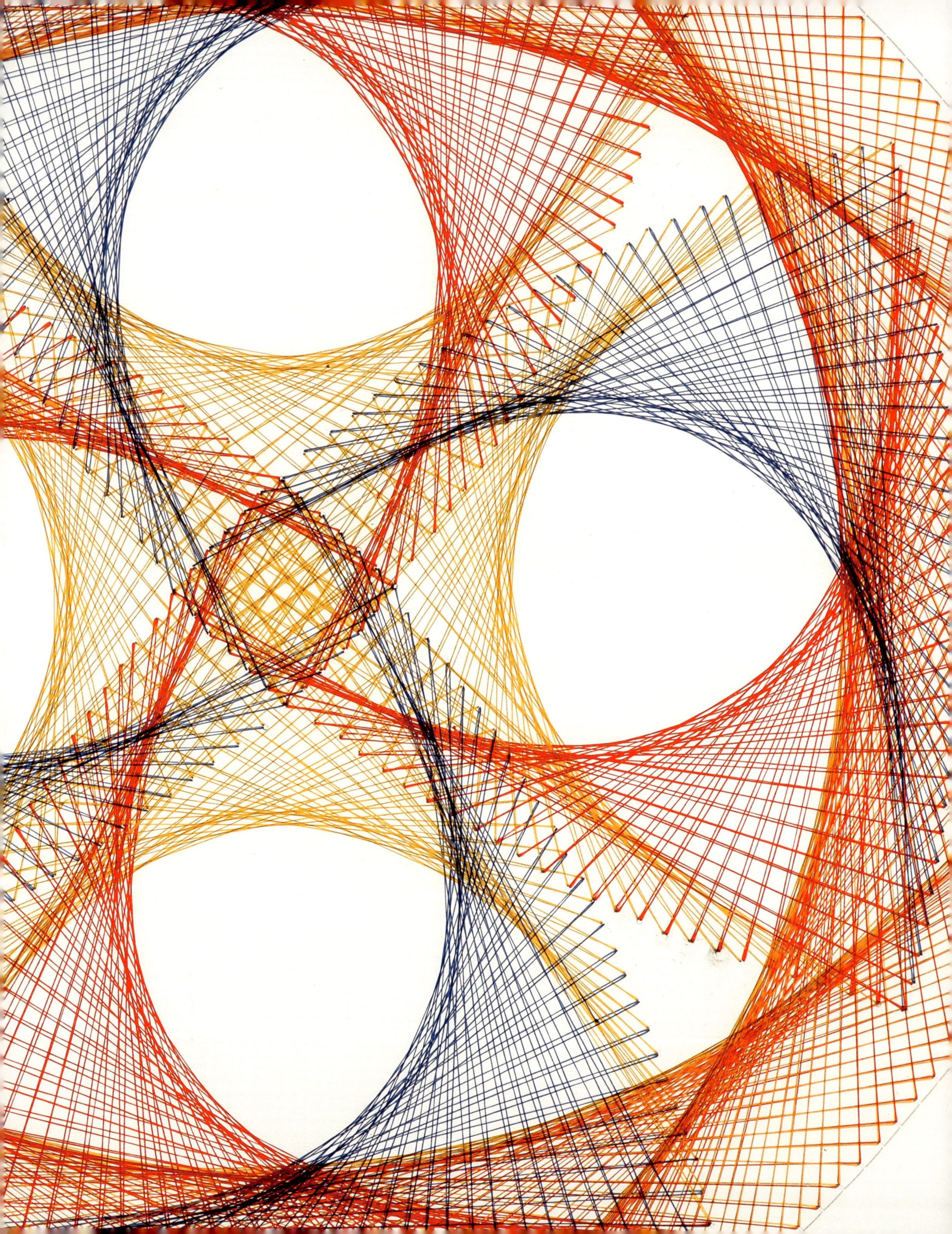

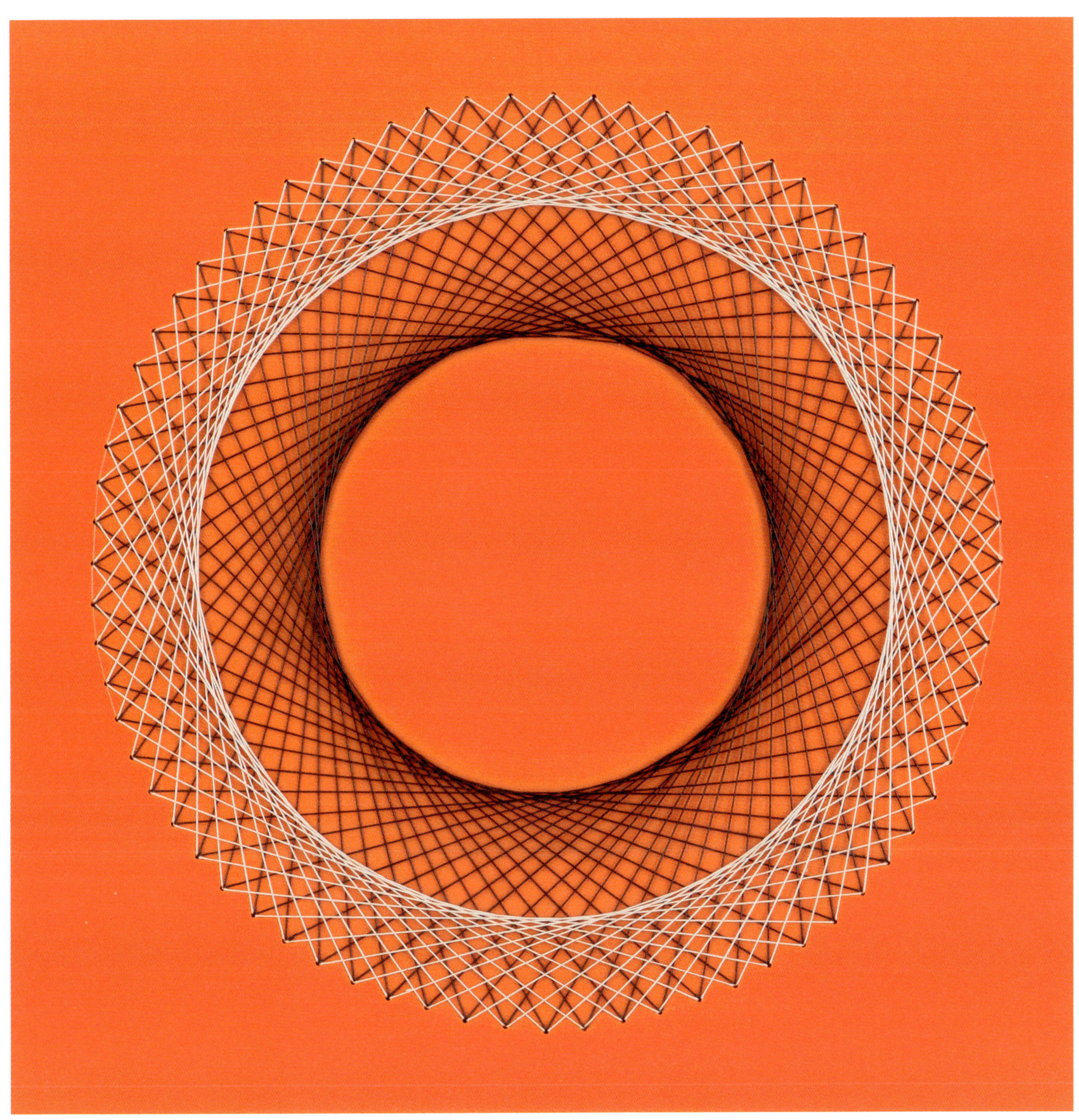

Sue Fuller, *String Composition*, c.1960s
Polypropylene thread on plexiglass, 11¾ × 11¾ in. (30 × 30 cm)

opposite:
Sue Fuller, *String Composition #554*, 1968 (detail)
Lucite and polypropylene thread, 26⅞ × 26⅞ × 1⅝ in. (68 × 68 × 4 cm)

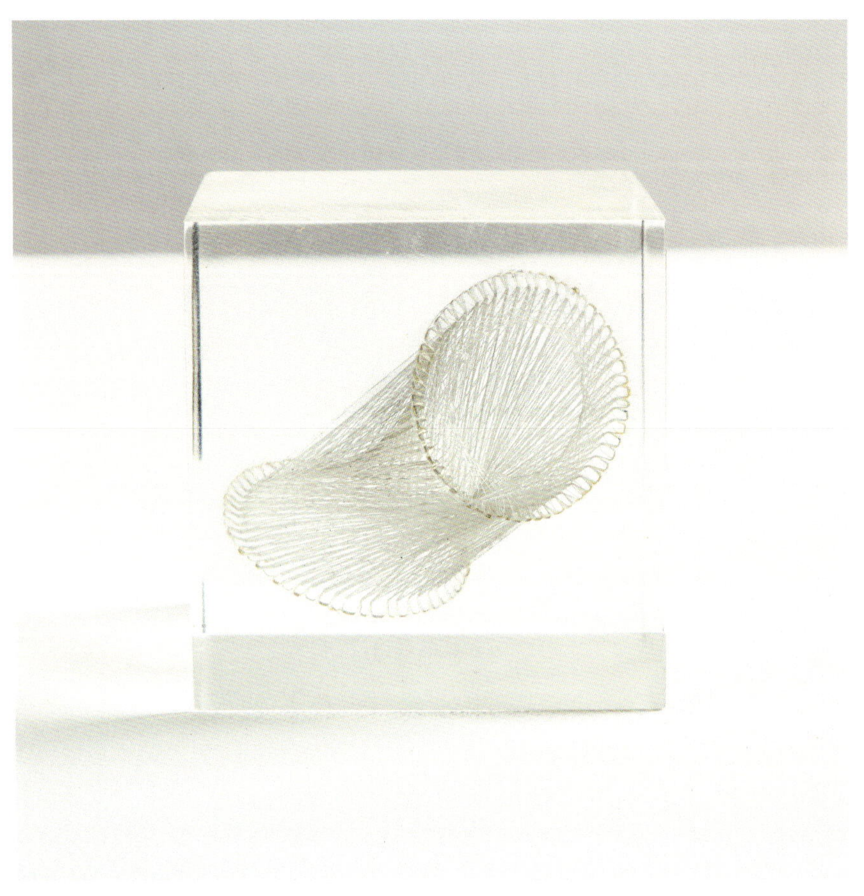

Sue Fuller, *String Composition '4×2'*, 1966
Lucite and polypropylene thread,
4 × 4 × 4 in. (10 × 10 × 10 cm)

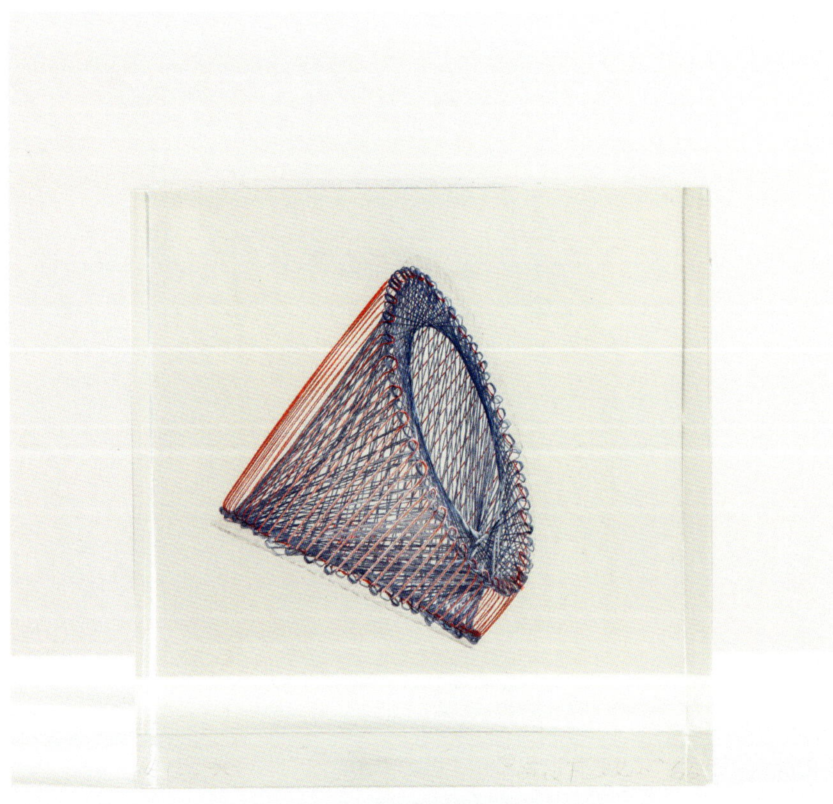

Sue Fuller, *String Composition #462*, 1966
Lucite and polypropylene thread,
5⅞ × 5⅞ × 5⅞ in. (15 × 15 × 15 cm)

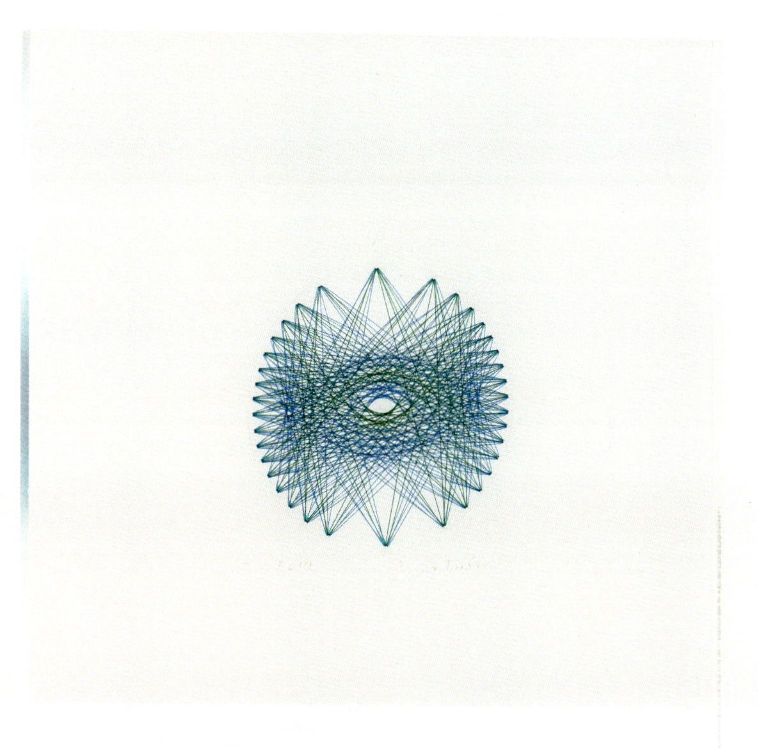

Sue Fuller, *String Composition #619*, 1968
Lucite and polypropylene thread,
12 × 12 × ¾ in. (30.5 × 30.5 × 2 cm)

Sue Fuller, *String Composition #621*, 1968
Lucite and polypropylene thread,
12 × 12 × ¾ in. (30.5 × 30.5 × 2 cm)

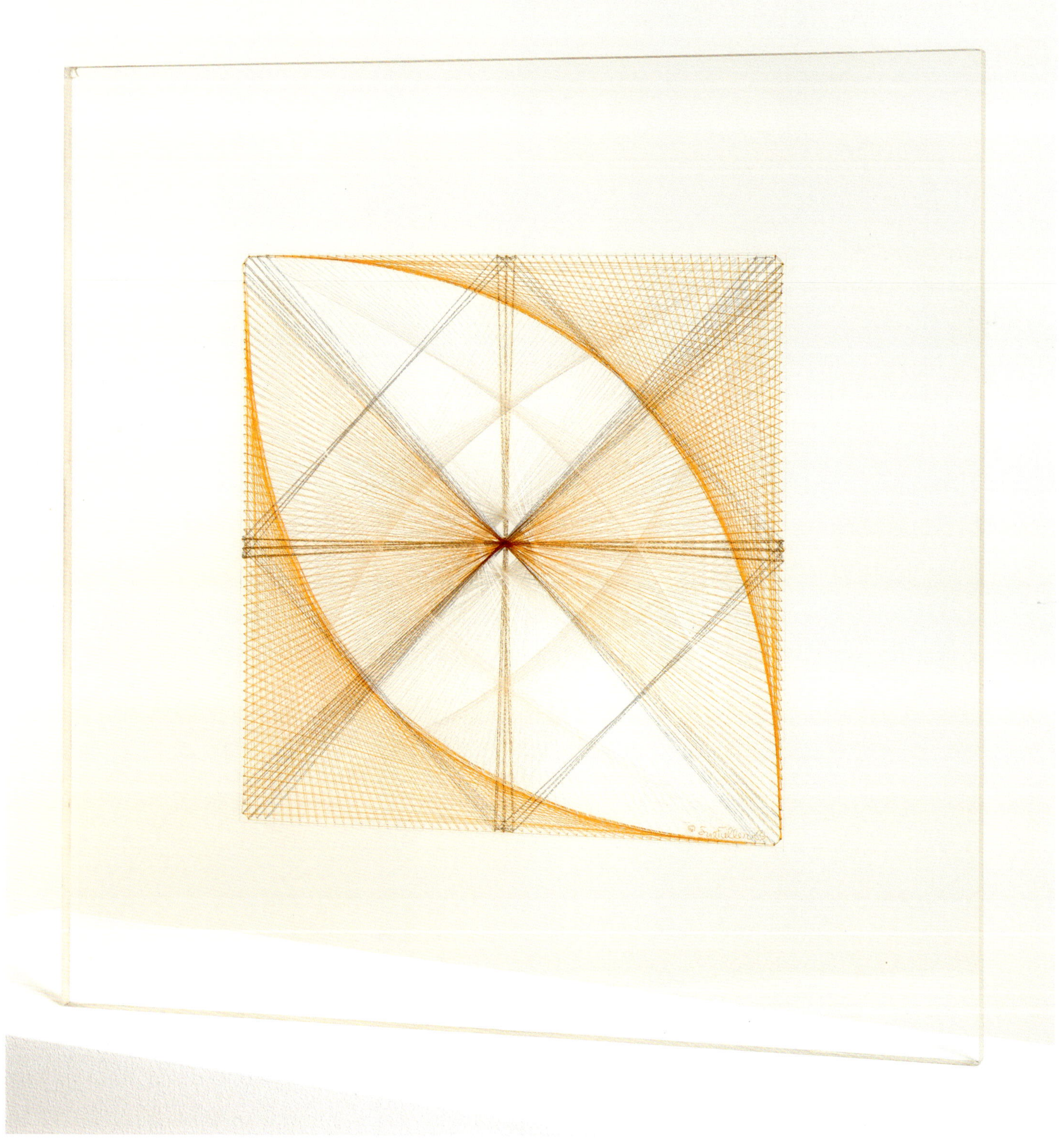

Sue Fuller, *String Composition #334*, 1965
Lucite and polypropylene thread, 25 × 25 × 1 in. (63.5 × 63.5 × 2.5 cm)

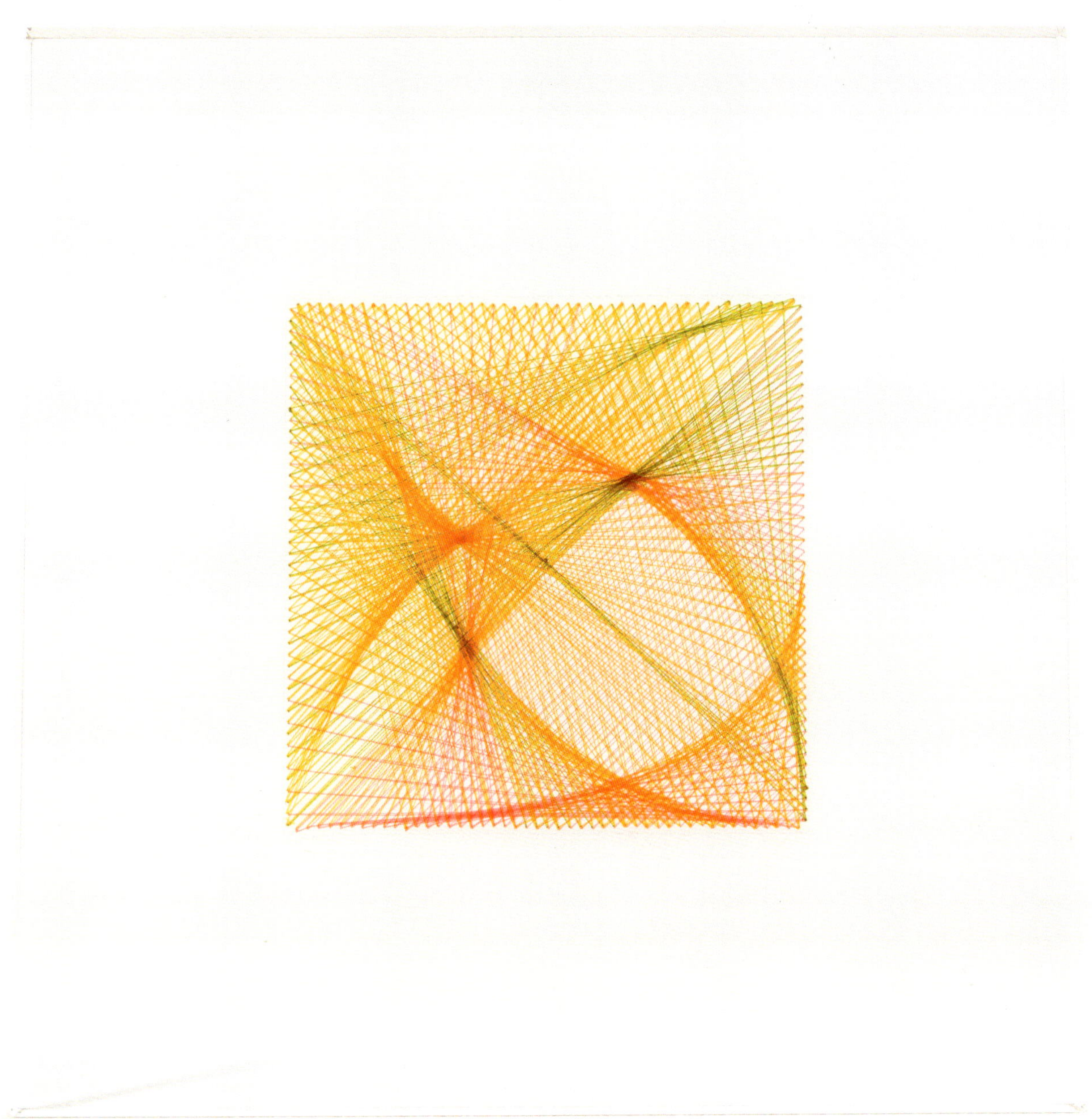

Sue Fuller, *String Composition #380*, 1970
Lucite and polypropylene thread, 12 × 12 × ¾ in. (30.5 × 30.5 × 2 cm)

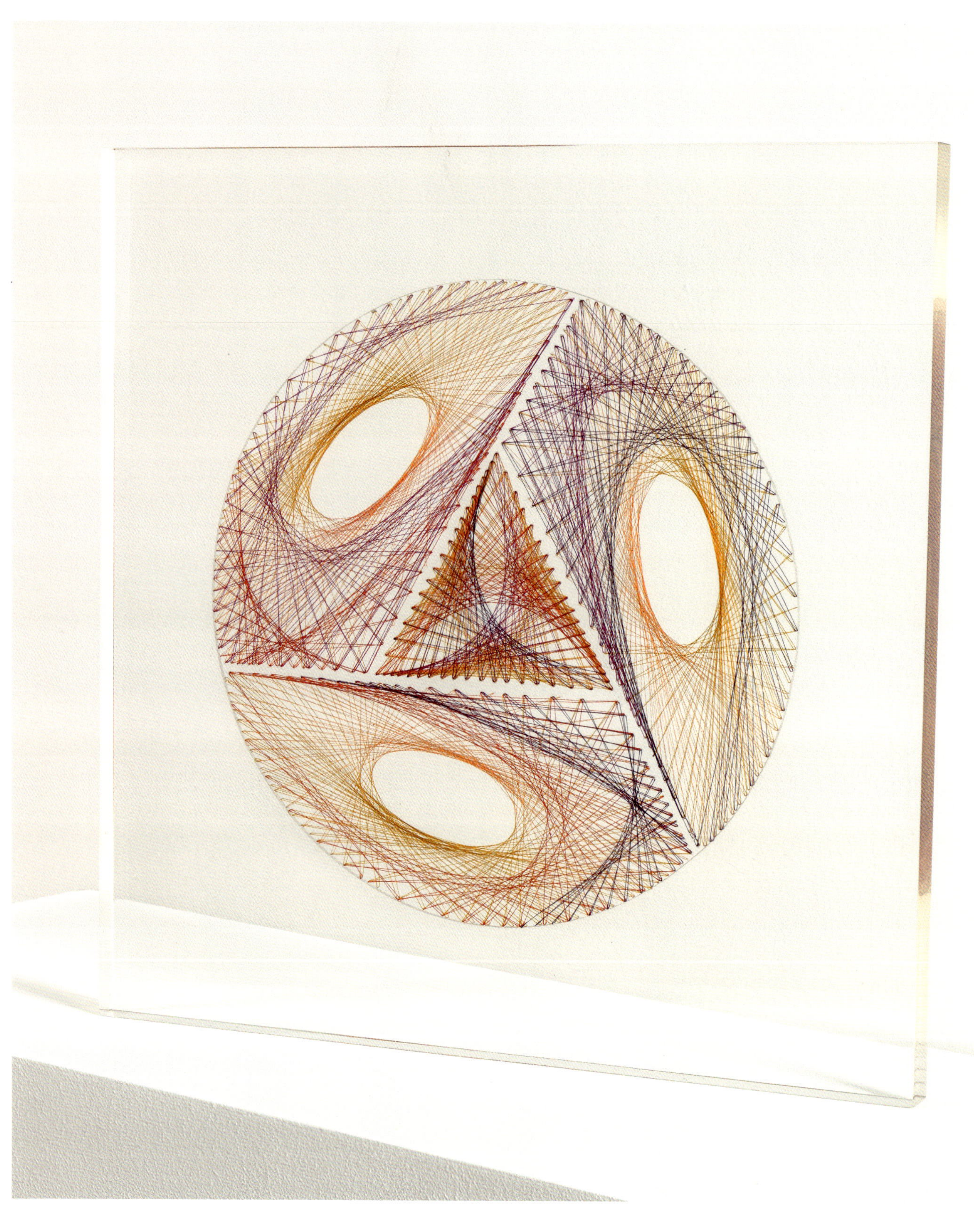

Sue Fuller, *String Composition #540*, 1969
Lucite and polypropylene thread, 21 × 21 × 1⅛ in. (53.5 × 53.5 × 3 cm)

opposite:
Sue Fuller, *String Composition #625*, 1969 (detail)
Lucite and polypropylene thread,
12 × 12 × ¾ in. (30.5 × 30.5 × 2 cm)

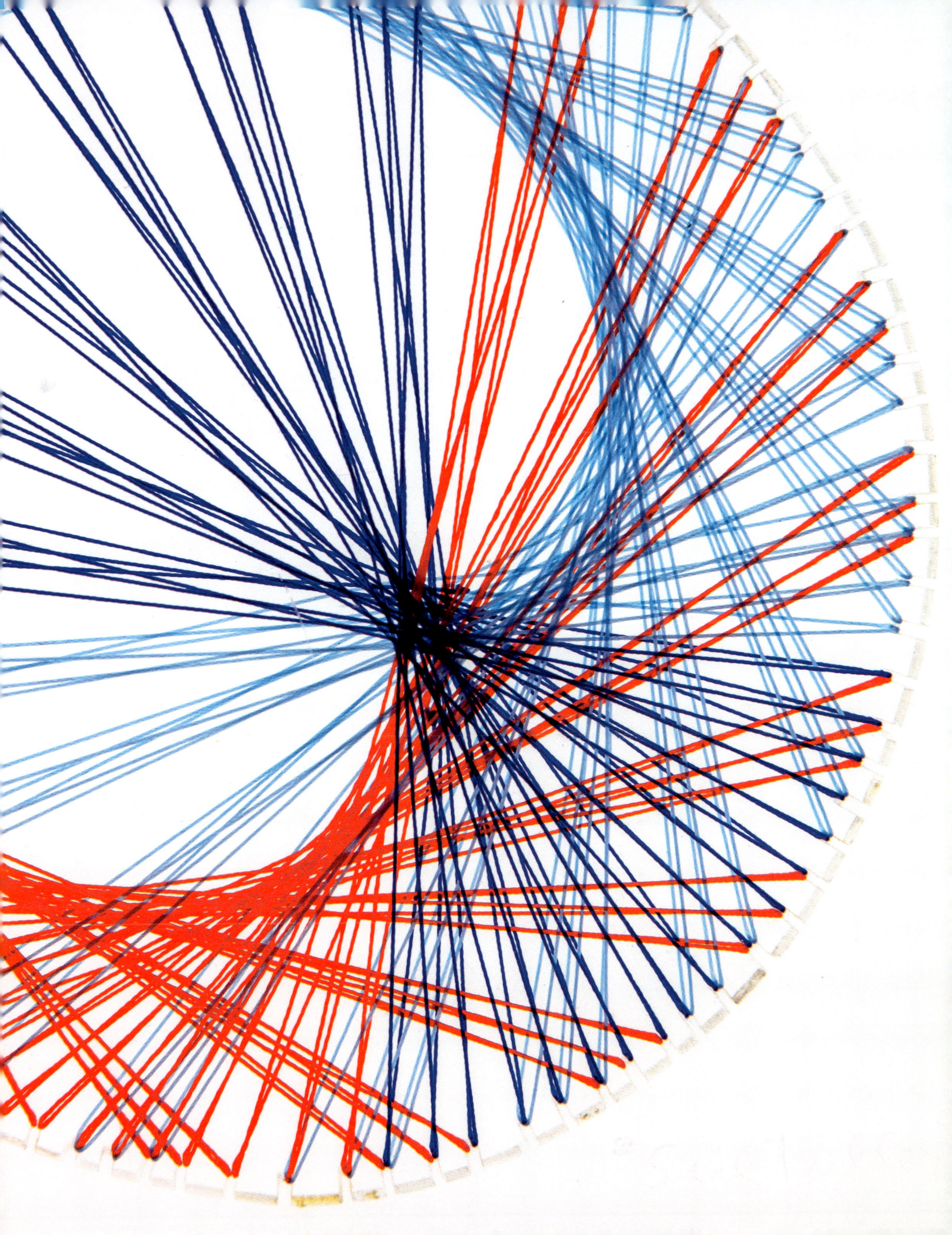

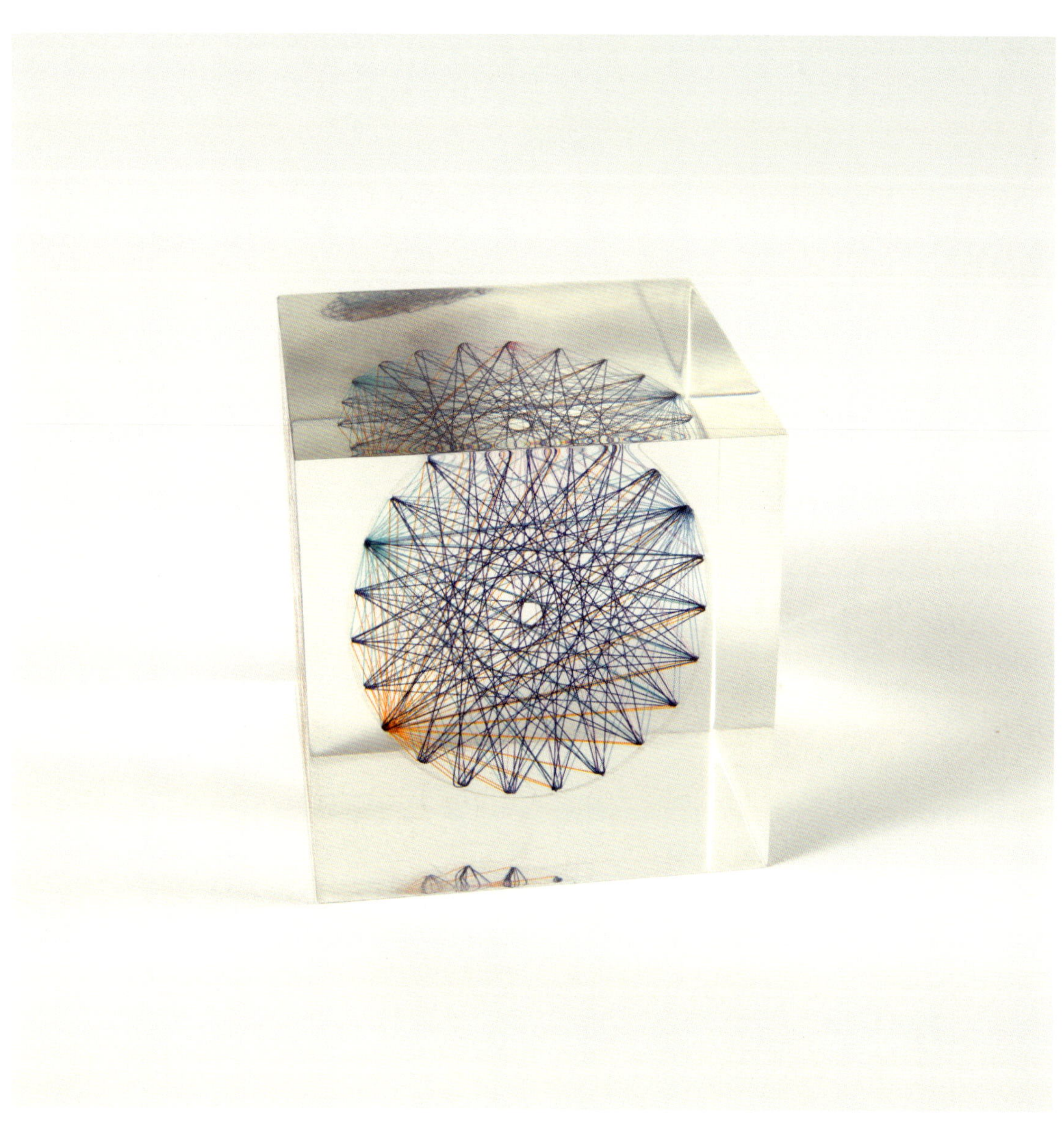

Sue Fuller, *String Composition #418*, 1969
Lucite and polypropylene thread, 5⅞ × 5⅞ × 5⅞ in. (15 × 15 × 15 cm)

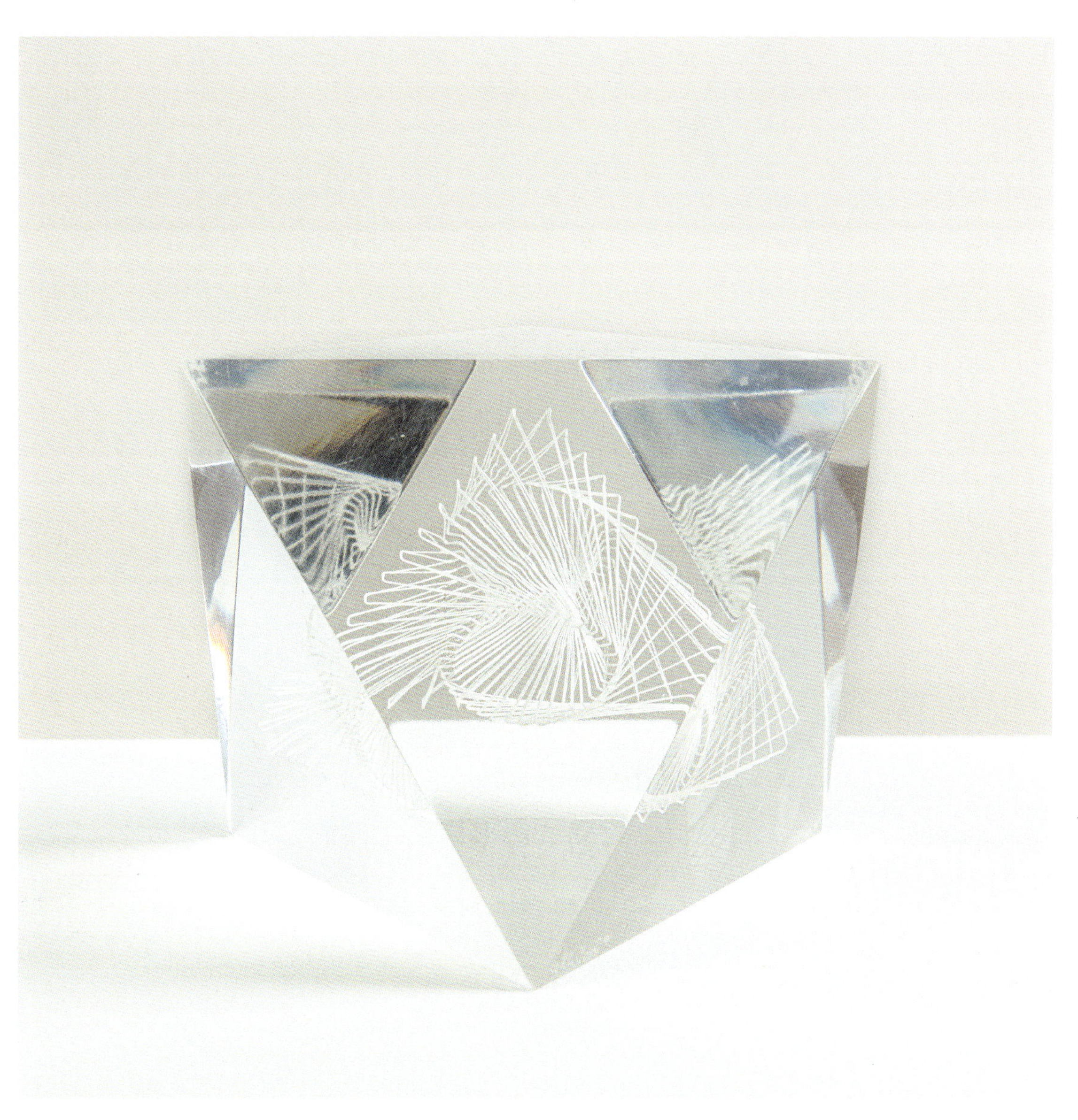

Sue Fuller, *String Composition #802*, 1969
Lucite and polypropylene thread, 6⅛ × 7½ × 8⅛ in. (15.5 × 19 × 20.5 cm)

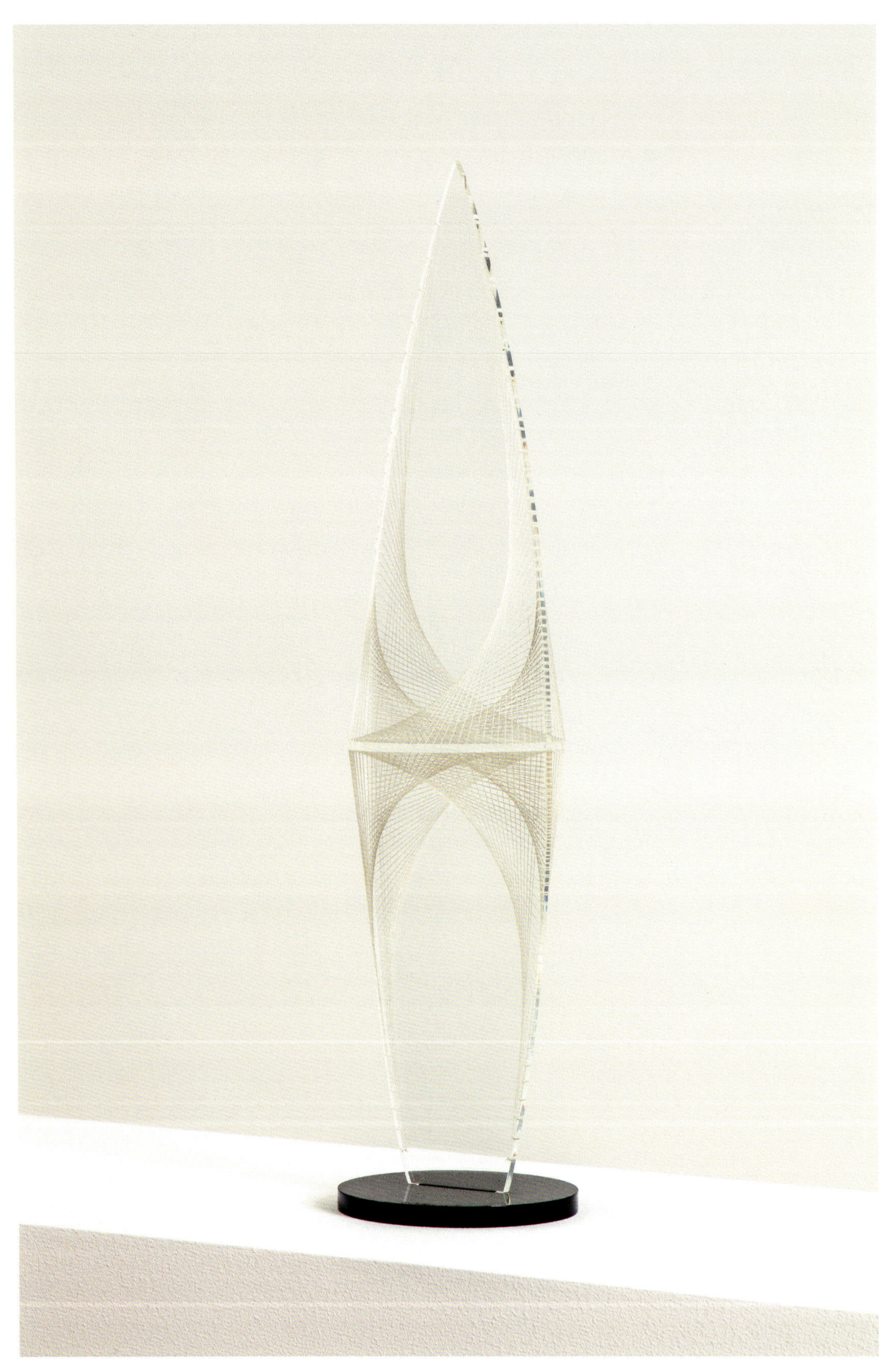

Sue Fuller, *Untitled*, 1969
Lucite and Teflon, 24¾ × 5⅞ × 5⅞ in. (63 × 15 × 15 cm)

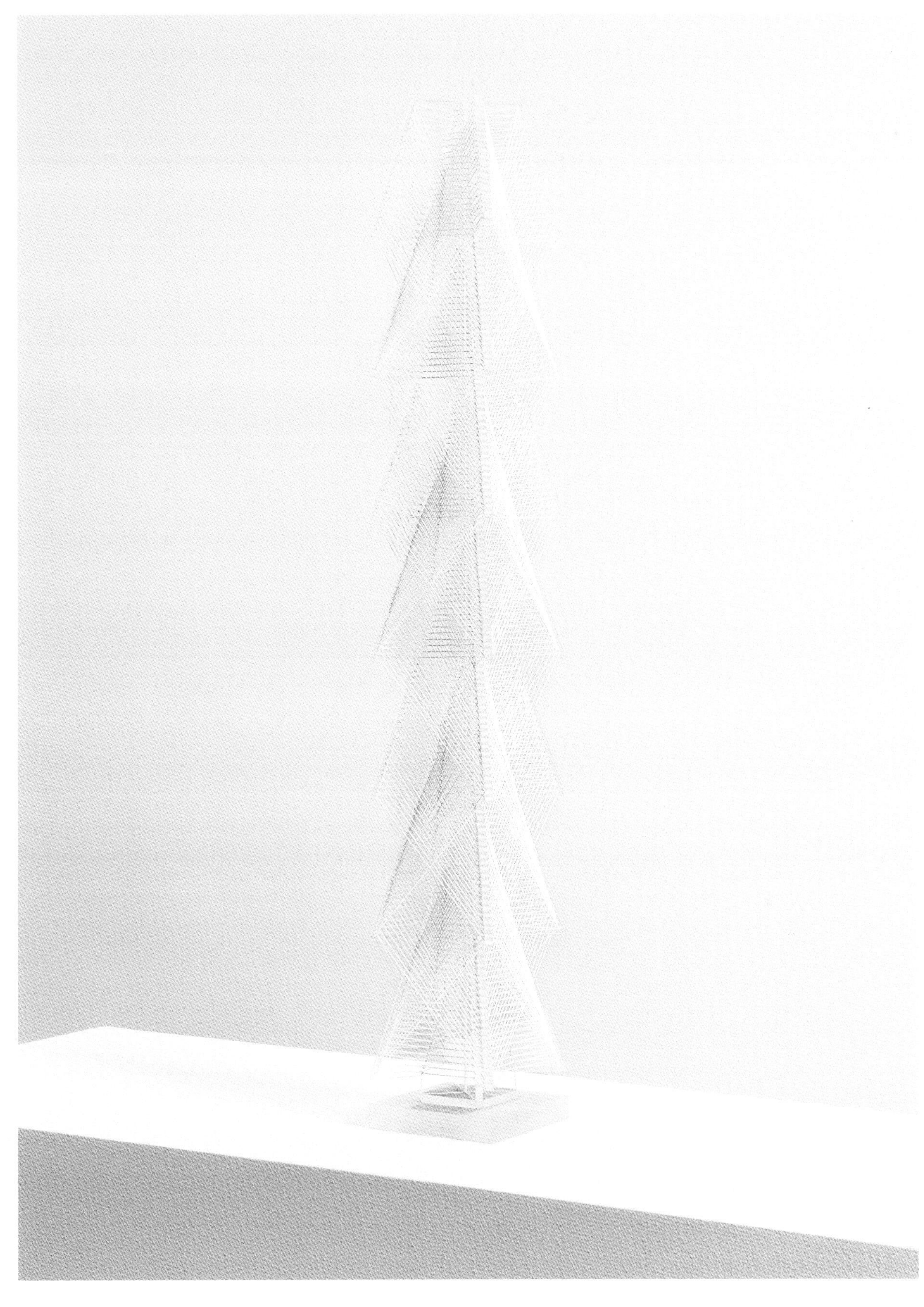

Sue Fuller, *White Pinnacle*, early 1960s
Lucite and Teflon, 29½ × 4½ × 4½ in. (75 × 11.5 × 11.5 cm)

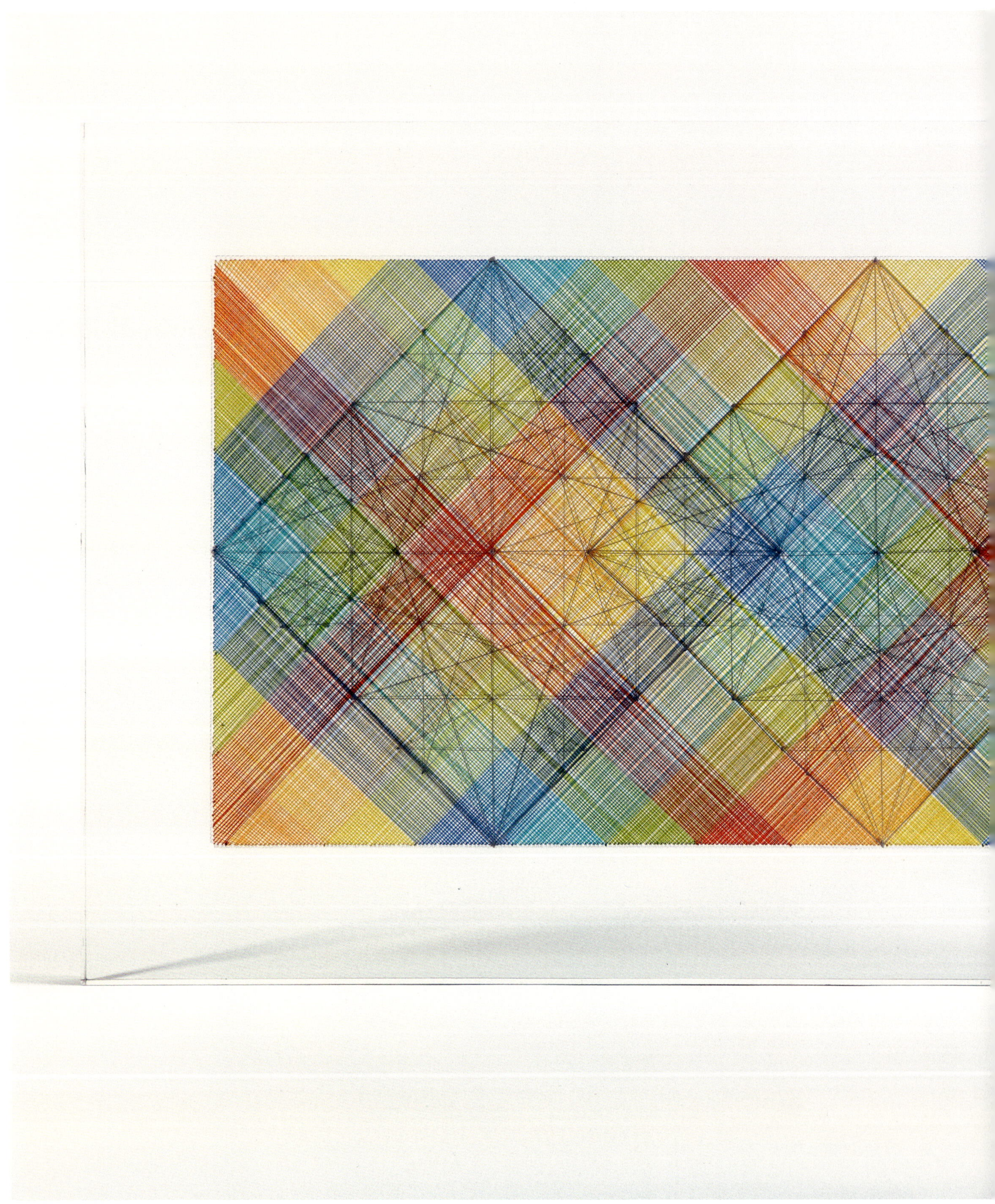

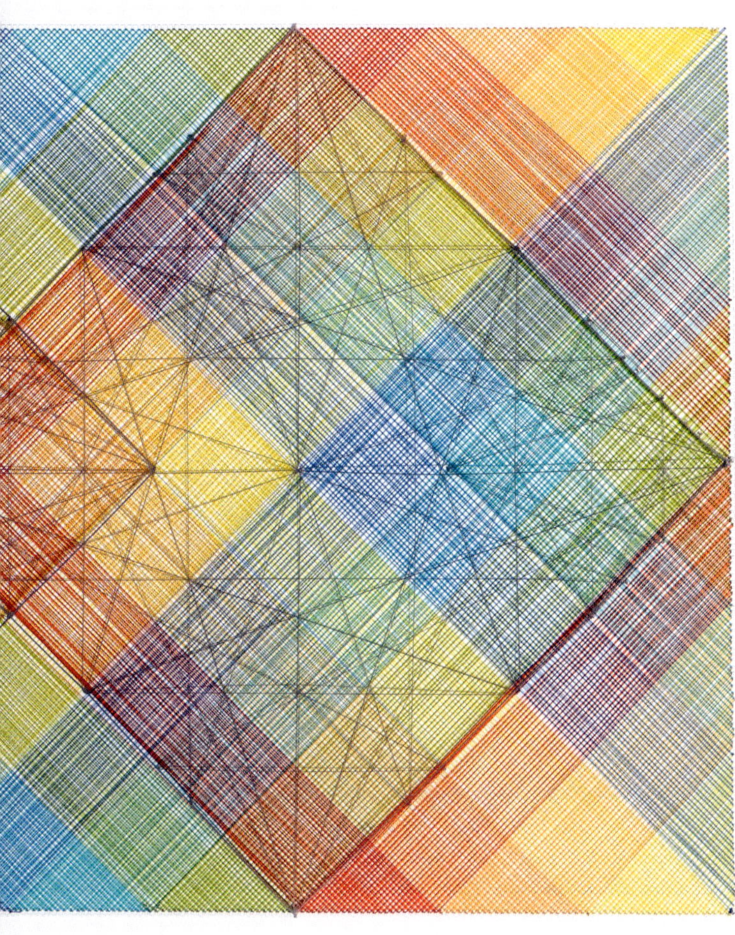

Sue Fuller, *Rectangle*, 1970
Lucite and polypropylene thread,
50 × 26 × 1¼ in. (127 × 66 × 3 cm)

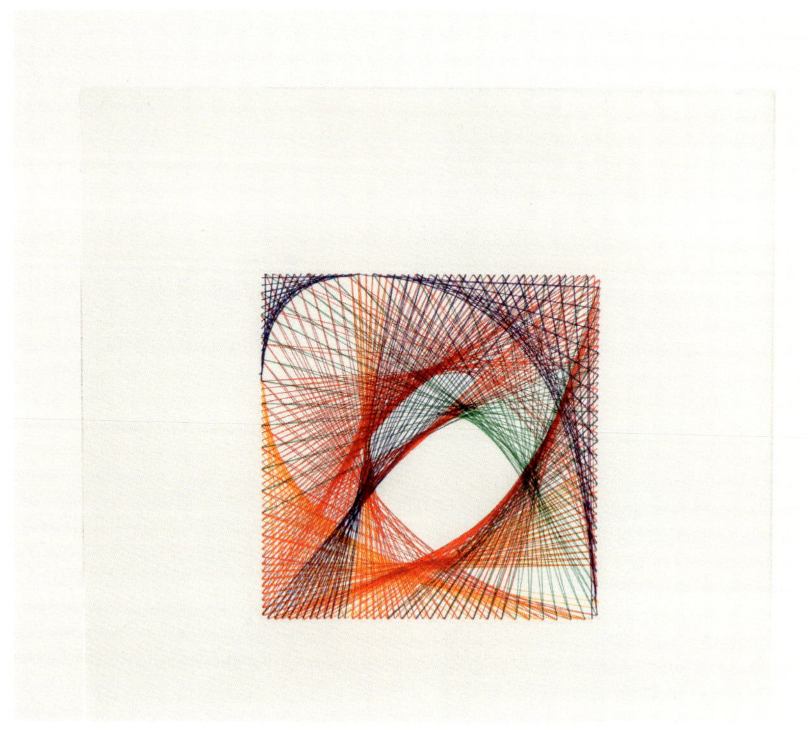

Sue Fuller, *String Composition #391*, 1971
Lucite and polypropylene thread,
12 × 12 × ¾ in. (30.5 × 30.5 × 2 cm)

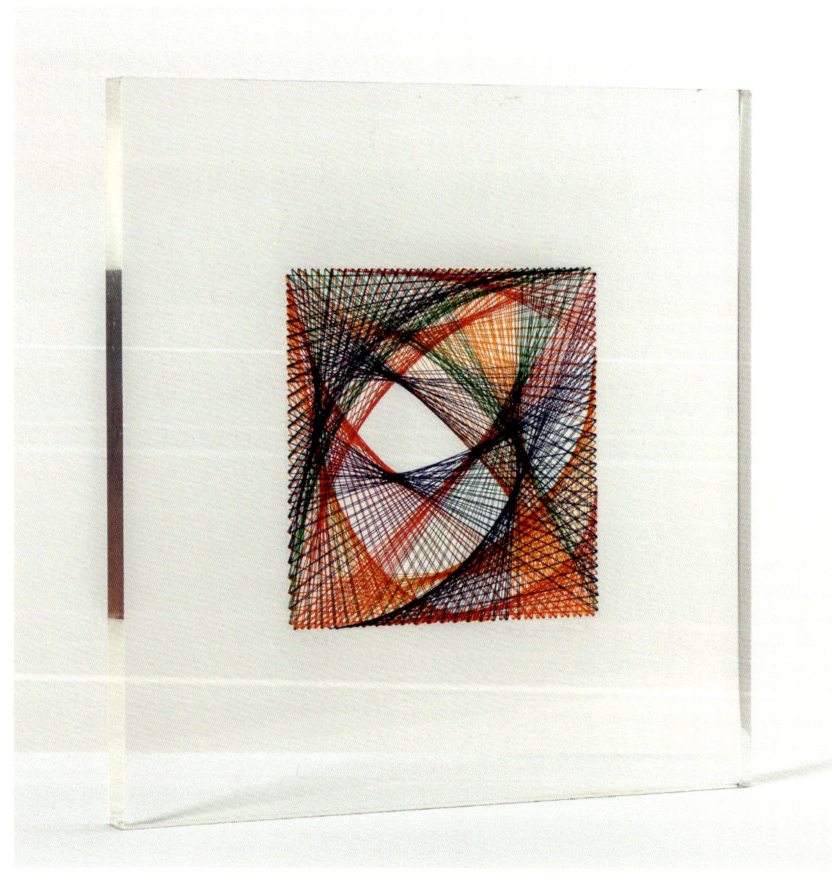

Sue Fuller, *String Composition #385*, 1971
Lucite and polypropylene thread,
12 × 12 × ¾ in. (30.5 × 30.5 × 2 cm)

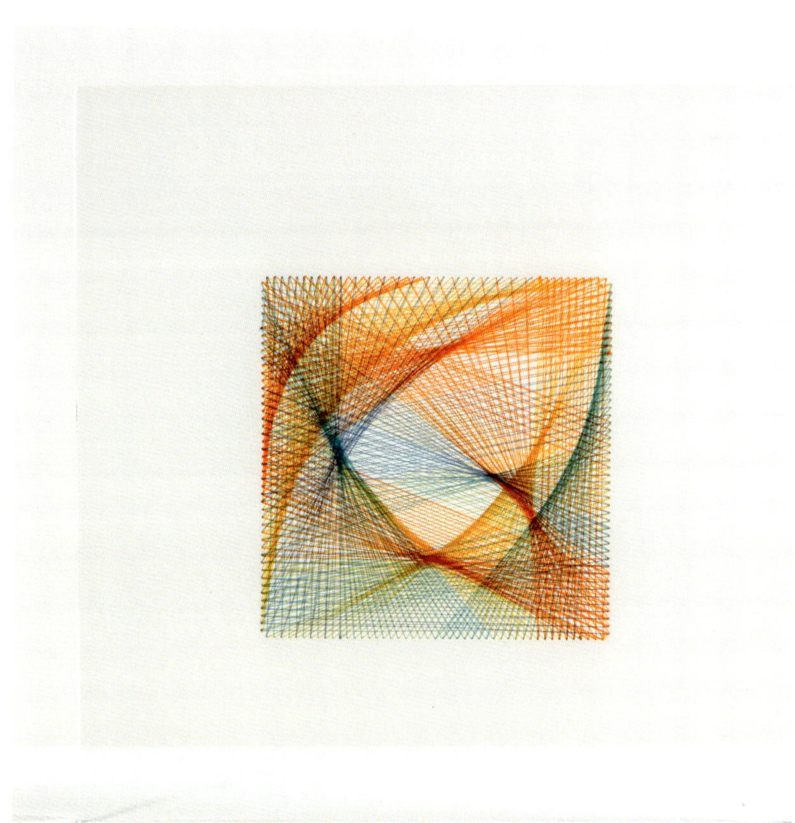

Sue Fuller, *String Composition #383*, 1971
Lucite and polypropylene thread,
12 × 12 × ¾ in. (30.5 × 30.5 × 2 cm)

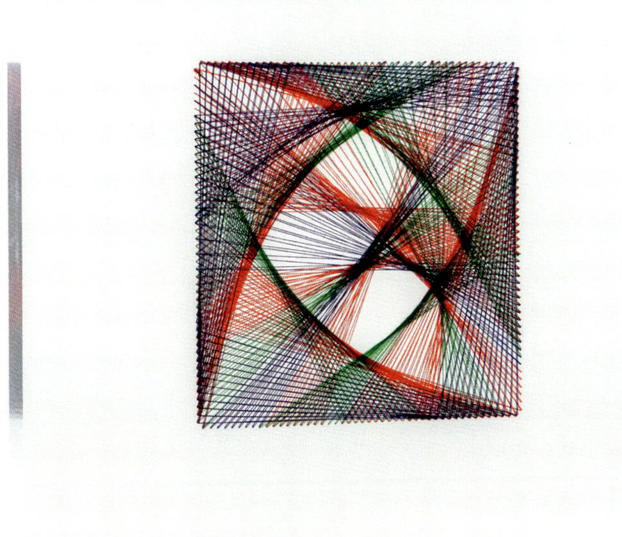

Sue Fuller, *String Composition #388*, 1971
Lucite and polypropylene thread,
12 × 12 × ¾ in. (30.5 × 30.5 × 2 cm)

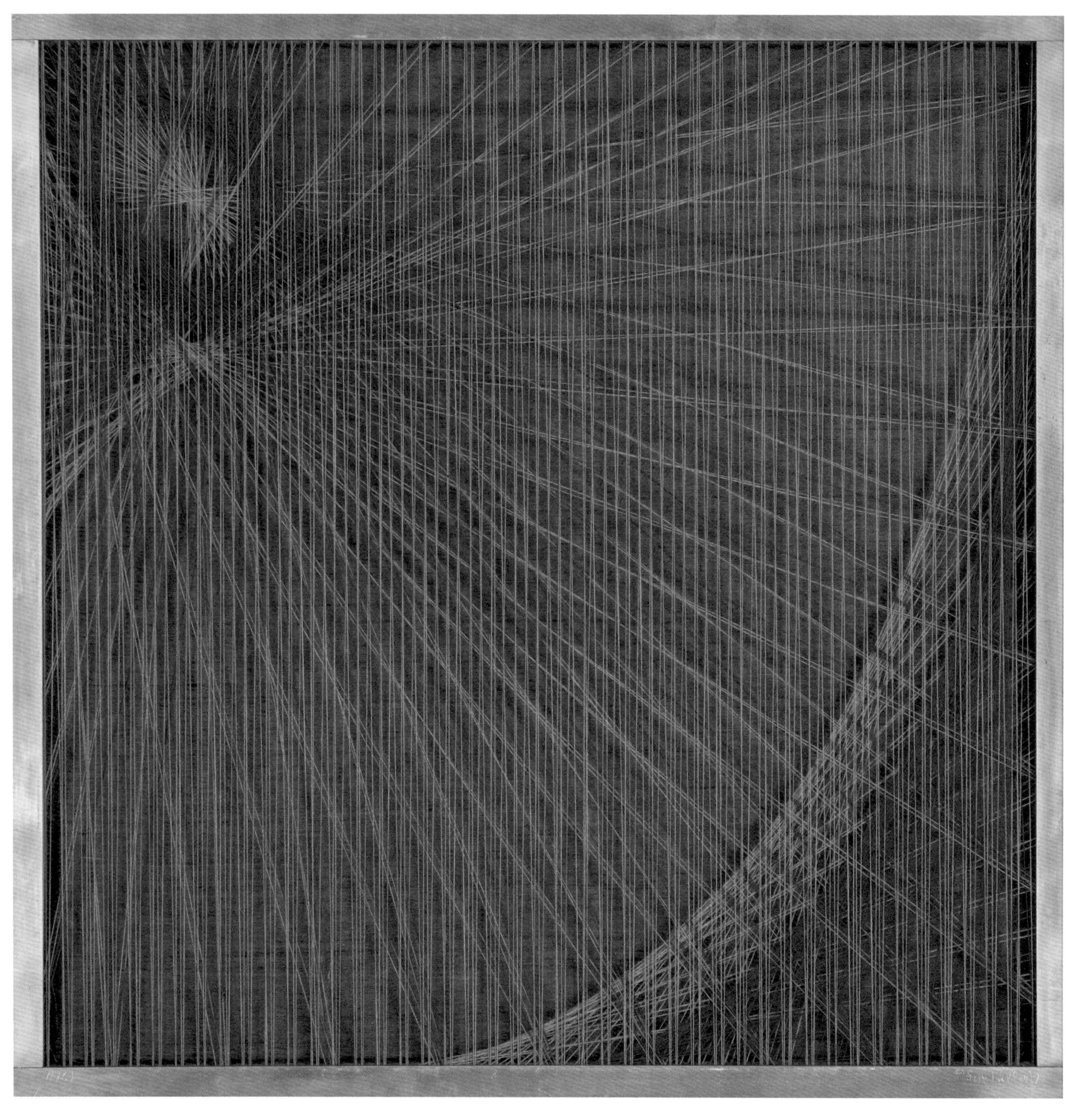

Sue Fuller, *String Composition #161 (We Will Harvest Infinity, Captain Ahab!)*, 1973
Polypropylene thread and fabric laid on canvas,
24⅜ × 24⅜ × 2 in. (62 × 62 × 5 cm)

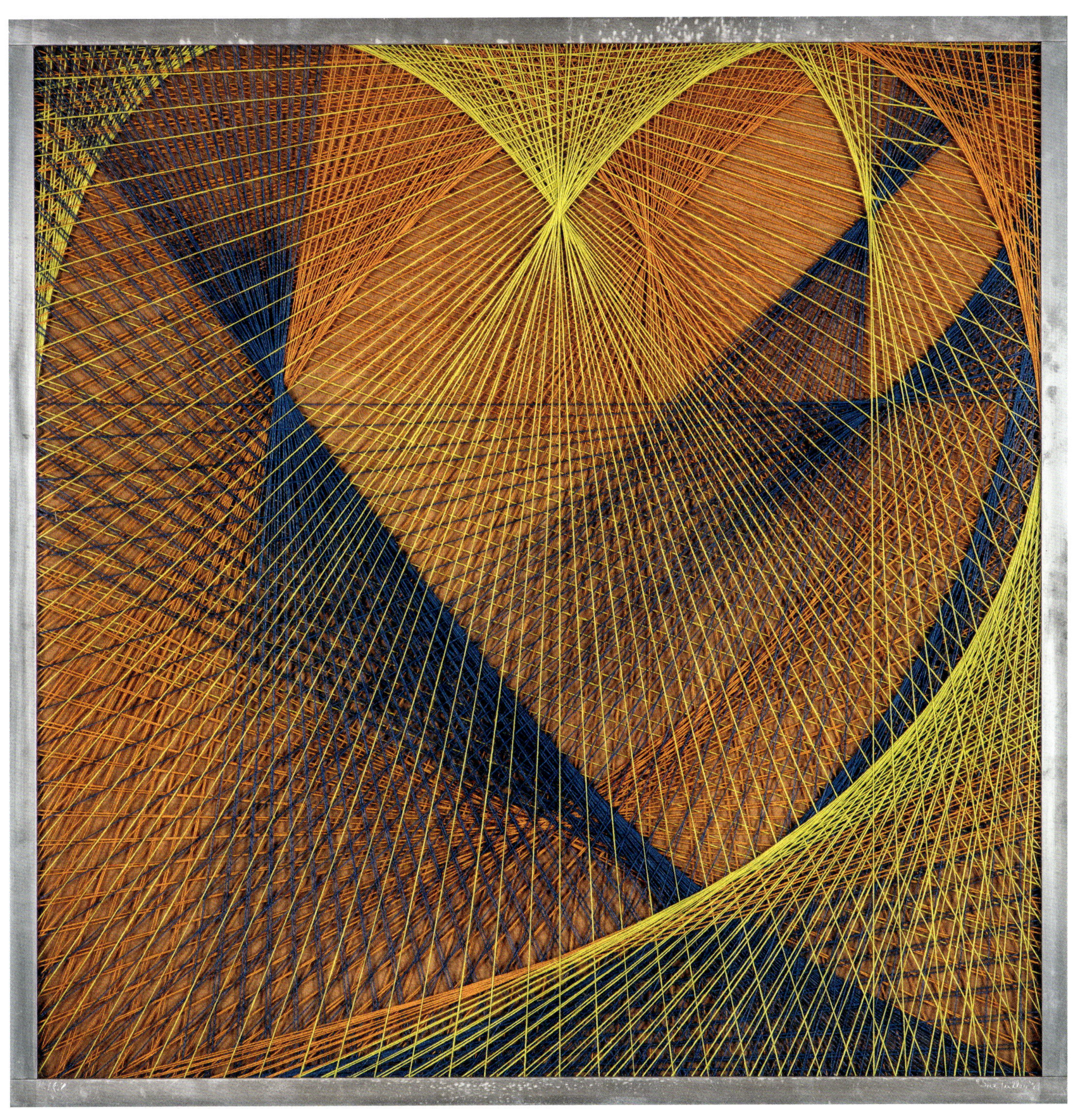

Sue Fuller, *String Composition #162*, 1974
Polypropylene thread and fabric laid on canvas,
35⅞ × 35⅞ × 2⅜ in. (91 × 91 × 6.5 cm)

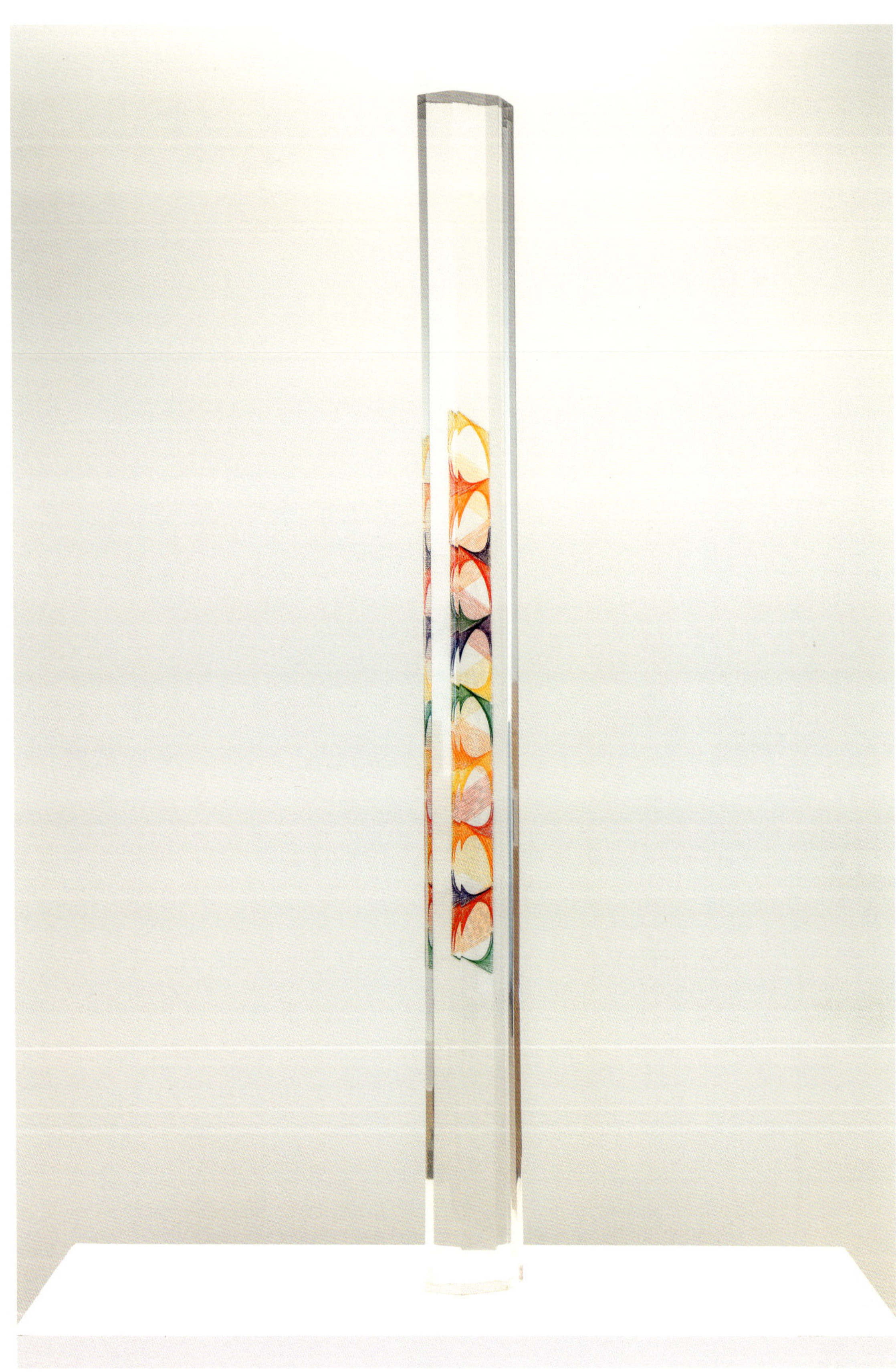

Sue Fuller, *Column*, c.1970
Lucite and polypropylene thread, 60 × 5½ × 2¾ in. (152.5 × 14 × 7 cm)

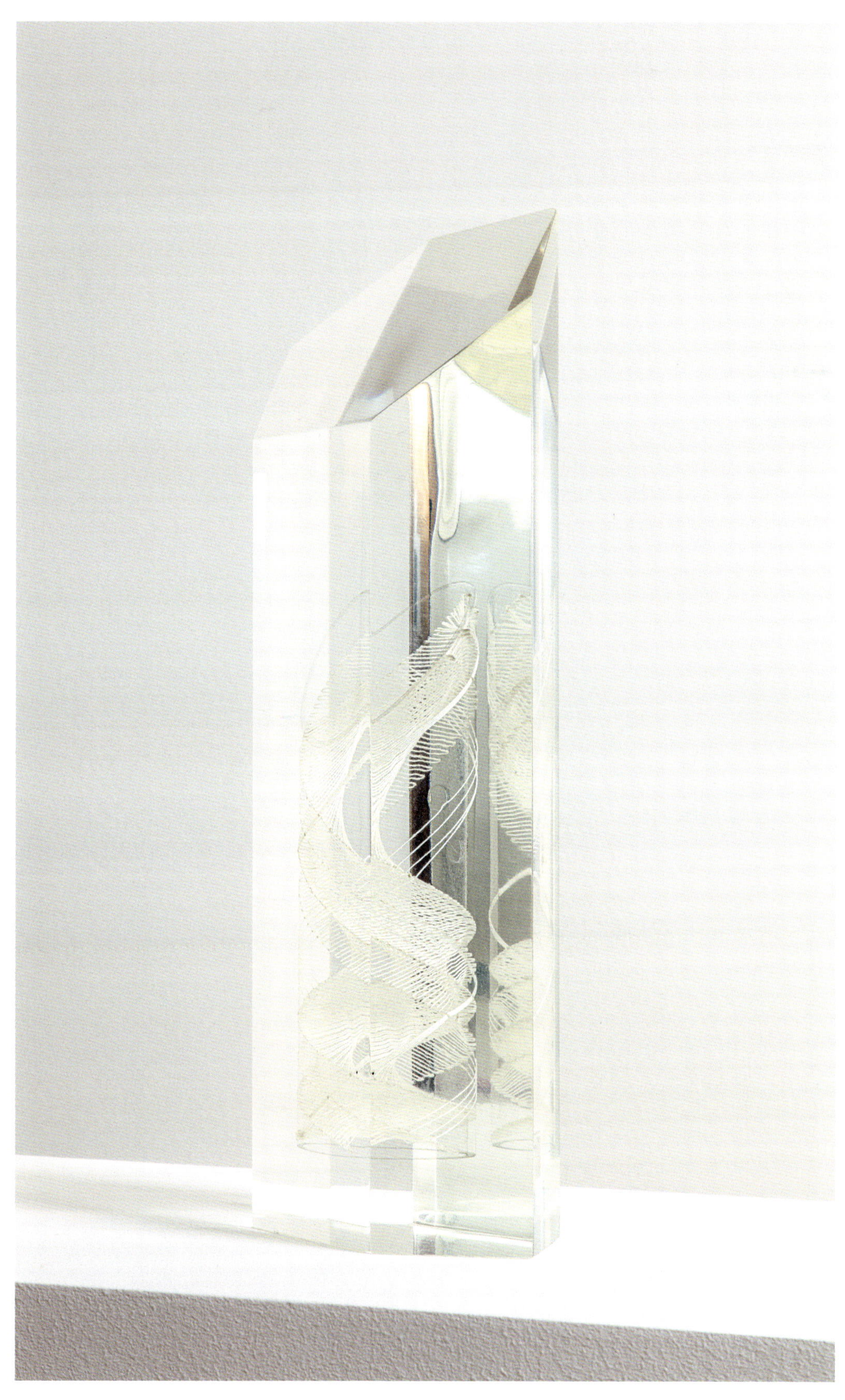

Sue Fuller, *String Composition #820*, 1974
Lucite and polypropylene thread, 18⅛ × 8⅛ × 4⅛ in. (46 × 20.5 × 10.5 cm)

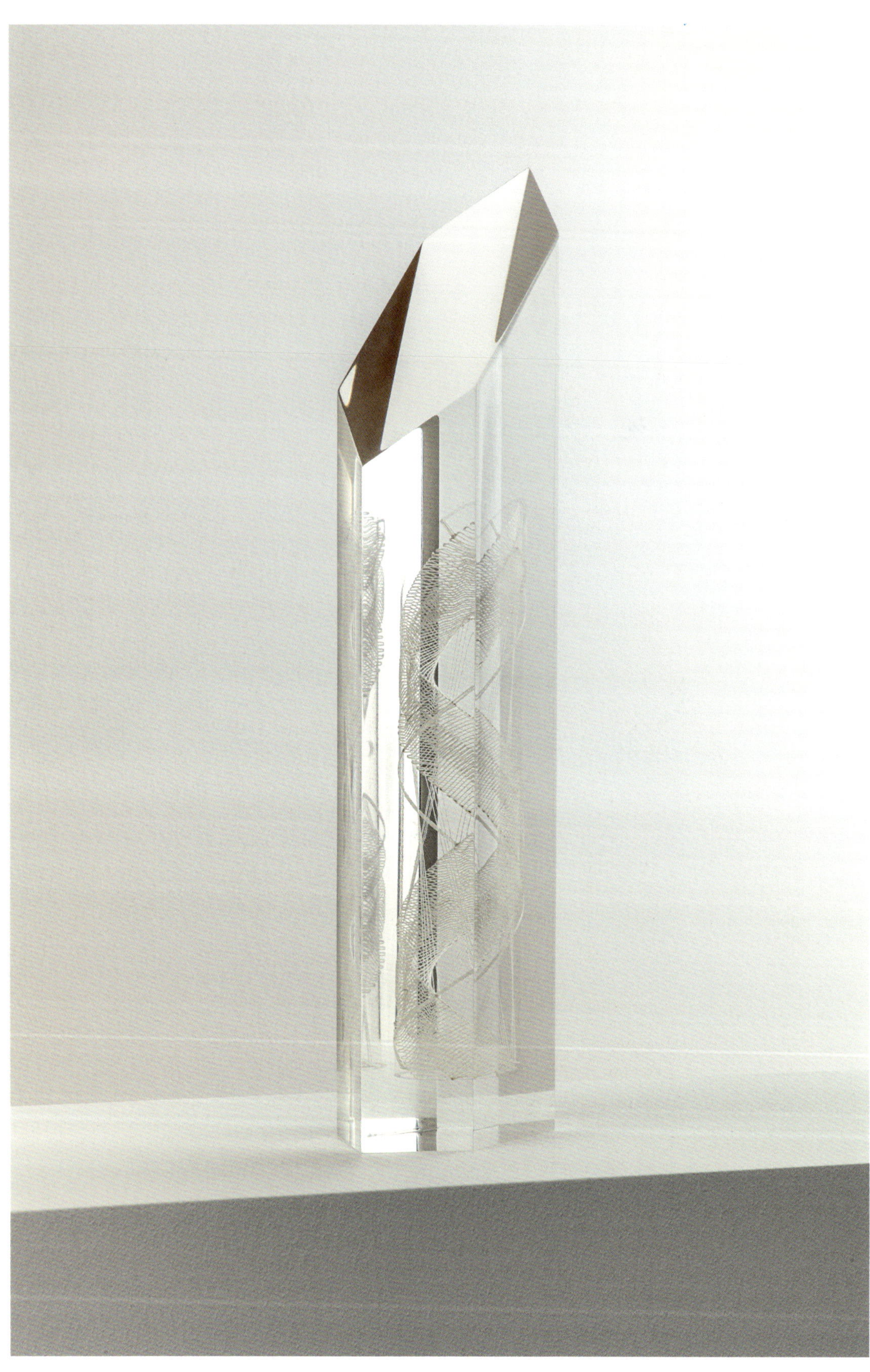

Sue Fuller, *String Composition #830*, 1974
Lucite and polypropylene thread, 23⅞ × 8⅛ × 4⅛ in. (60.5 × 20.5 × 10.5 cm)

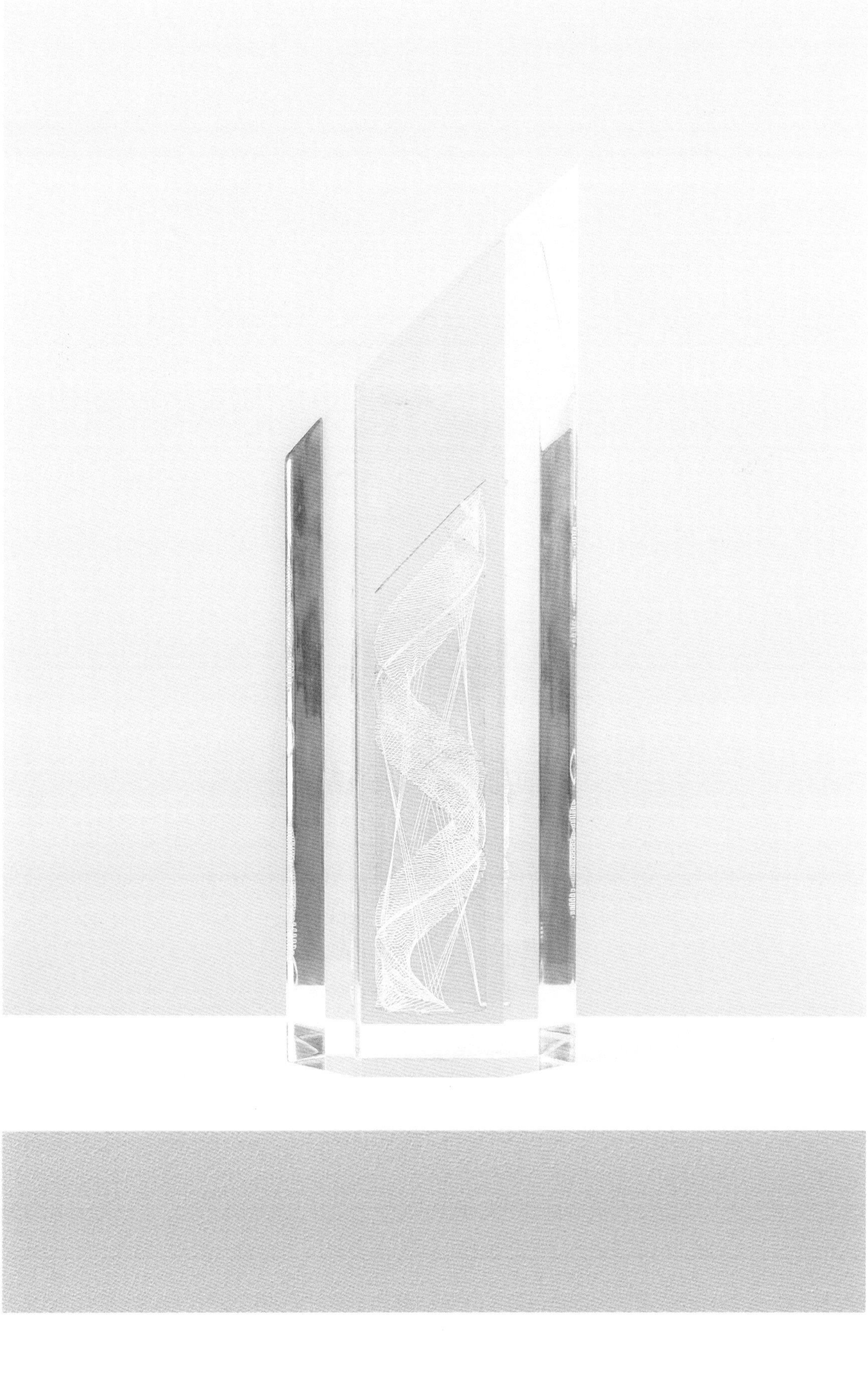

Sue Fuller, *String Composition #821*, 1974
Lucite and polypropylene thread, 17⅞ × 8⅛ × 4⅛ in. (45.5 × 20.5 × 10.5 cm)

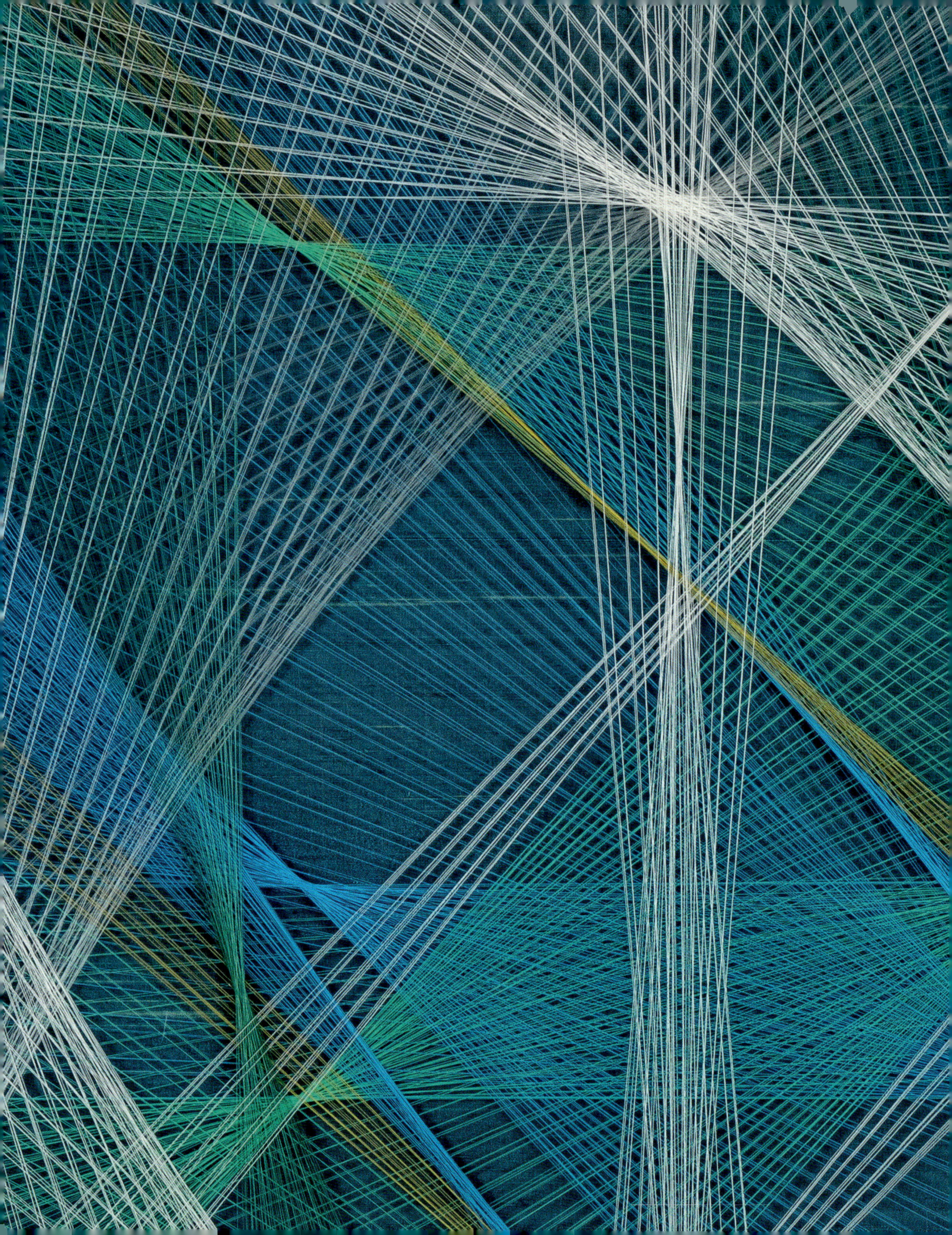

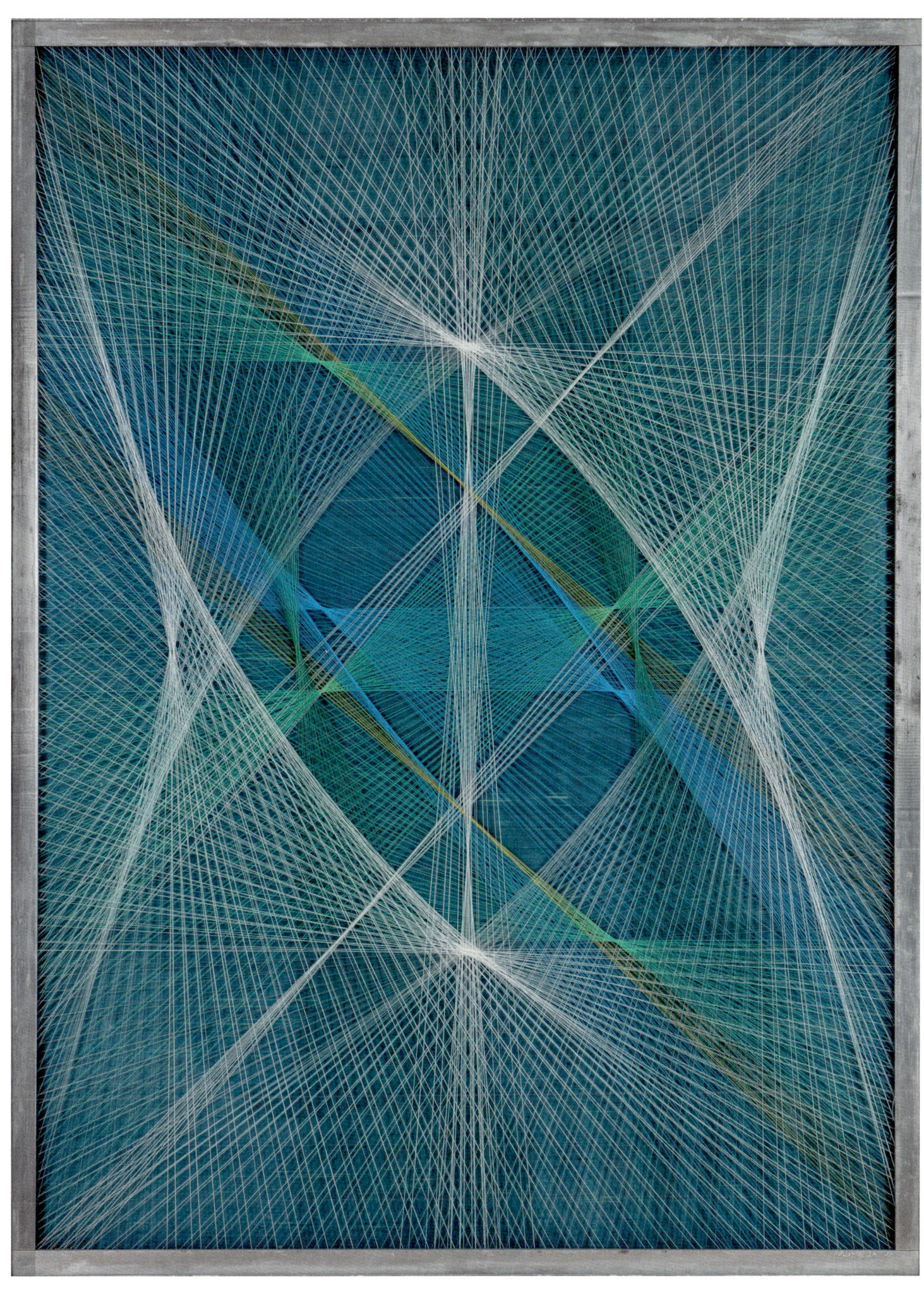

Sue Fuller, *String Composition #165*, 1975
Thread and fabric laid on canvas, 48⅜ × 36⅜ × 2 in. (123 × 92.5 × 5 cm)

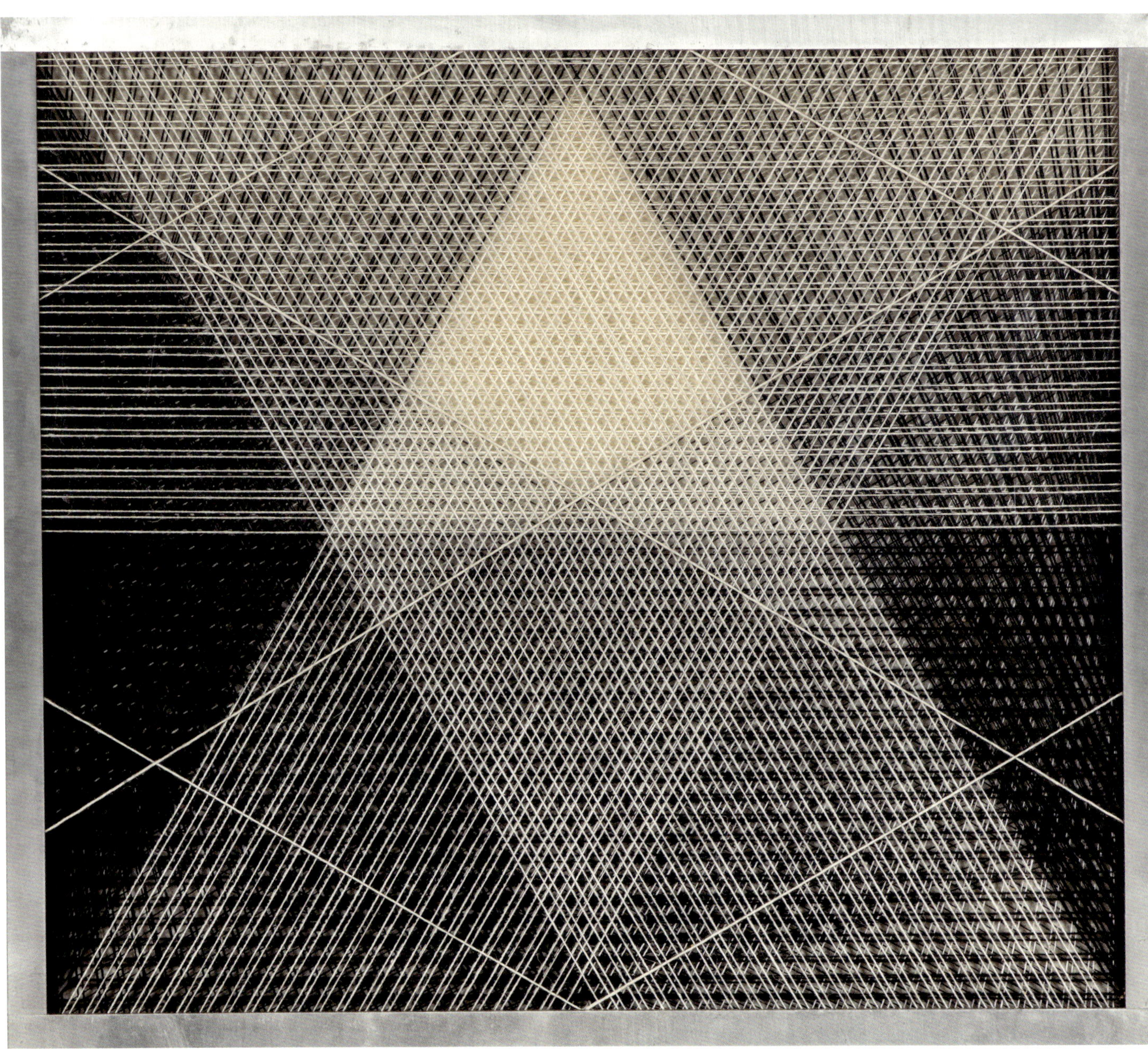

Sue Fuller, *String Composition #173*, 1976
Thread on canvas, 26⅜ × 30 × 2 in. (67 × 76.5 × 5 cm)

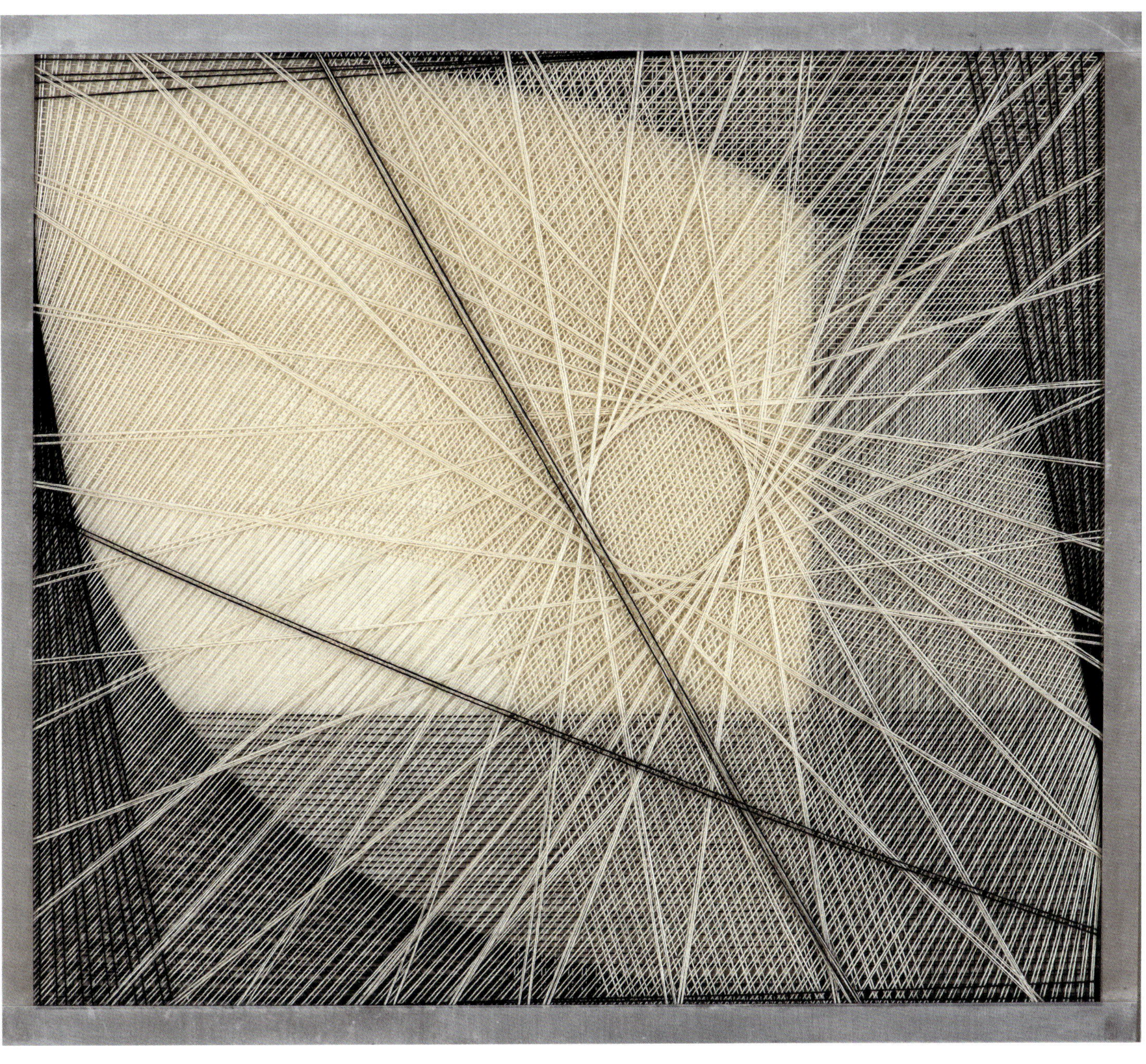

Sue Fuller, *String Composition #186*, 1978–81
Thread on canvas, 44 × 50 × 2½ in. (112 × 127 × 6.5 cm)

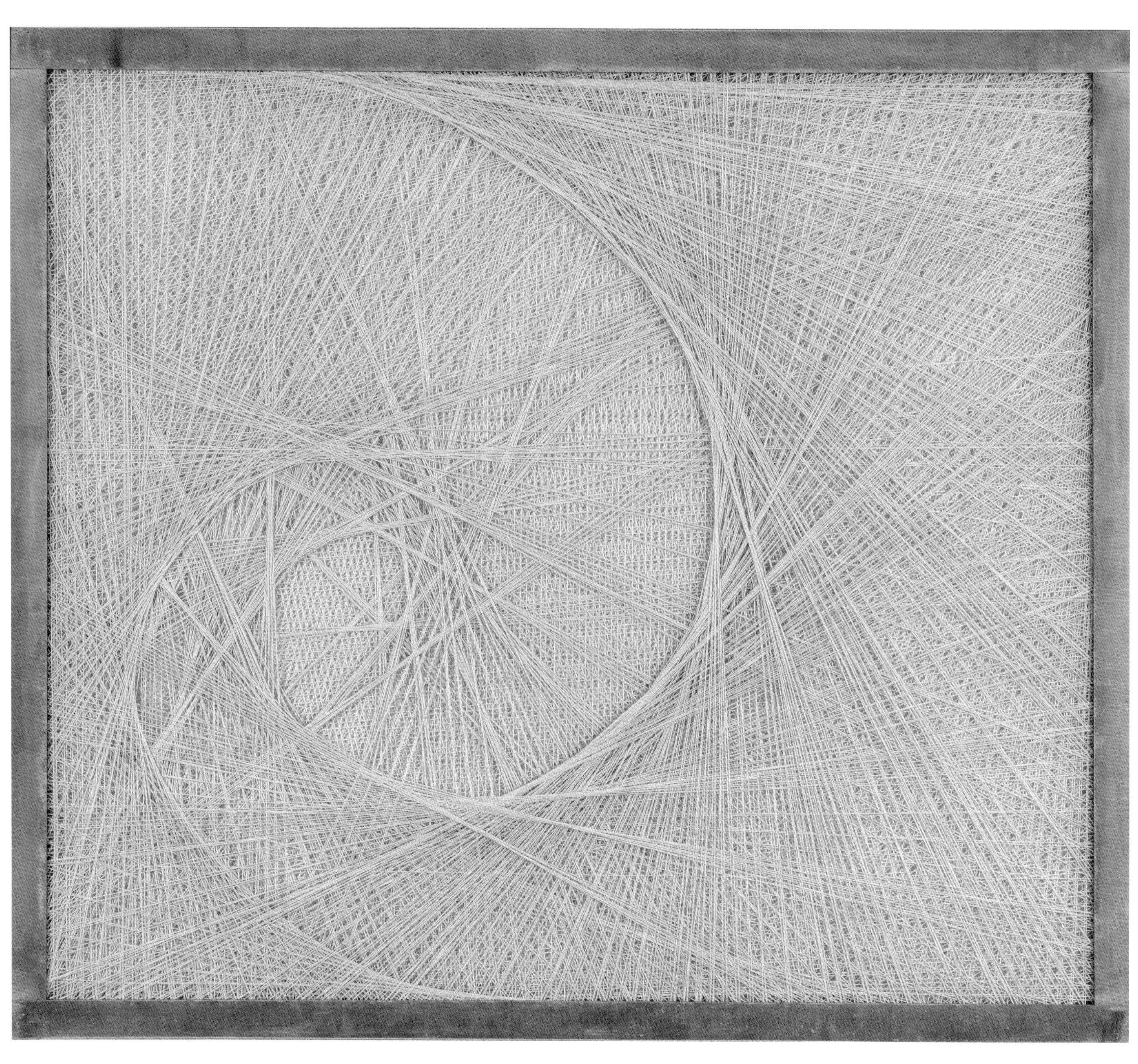

Sue Fuller, *String Composition #184*, 1978
Thread on canvas, 44 × 50 × 2½ in. (112 × 127 × 6.5 cm)

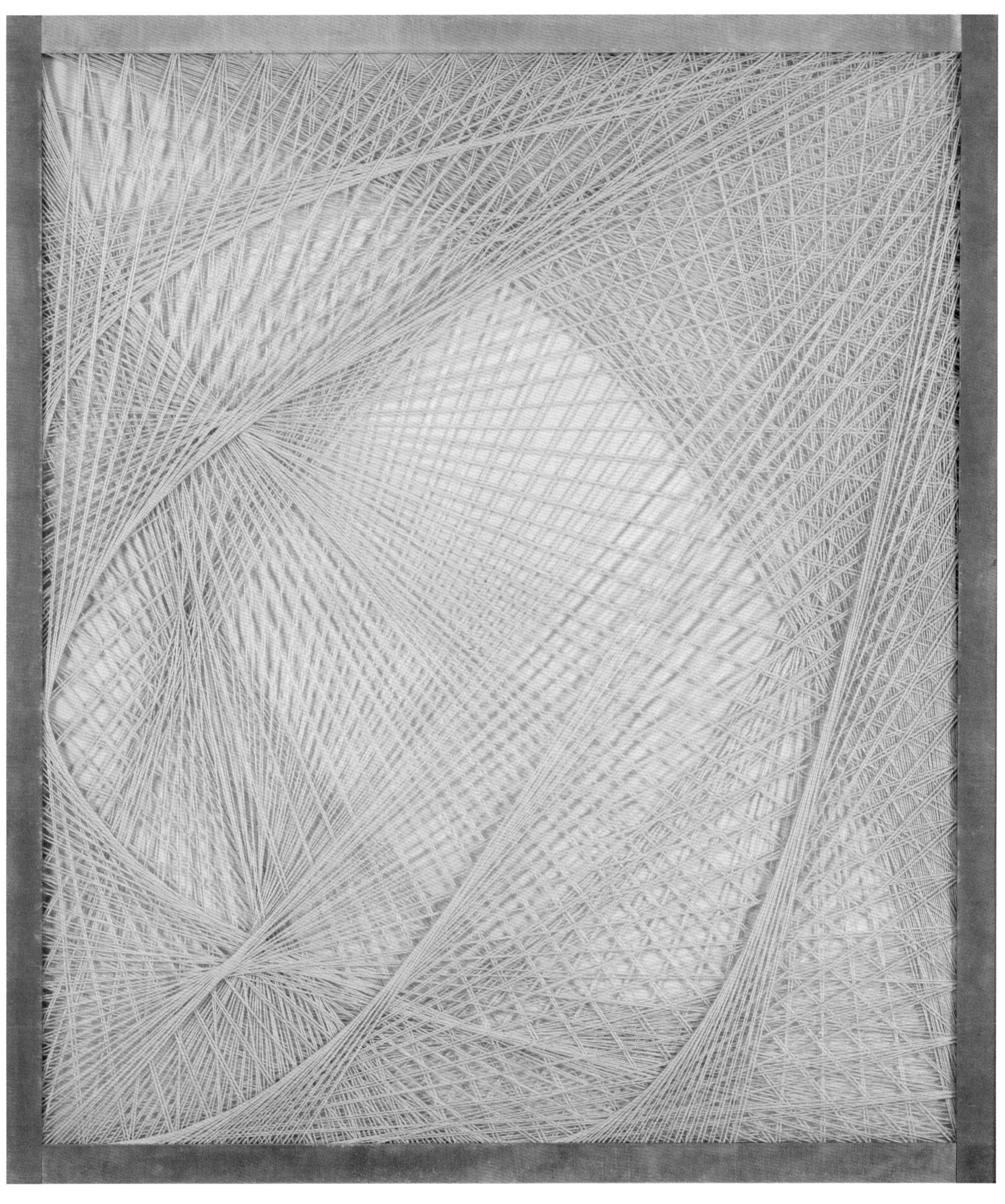

Sue Fuller, *String Composition #175*, 1976
Thread on canvas, 50 × 43⅞ × 2½ in. (127 × 111.5 × 6.5 cm)

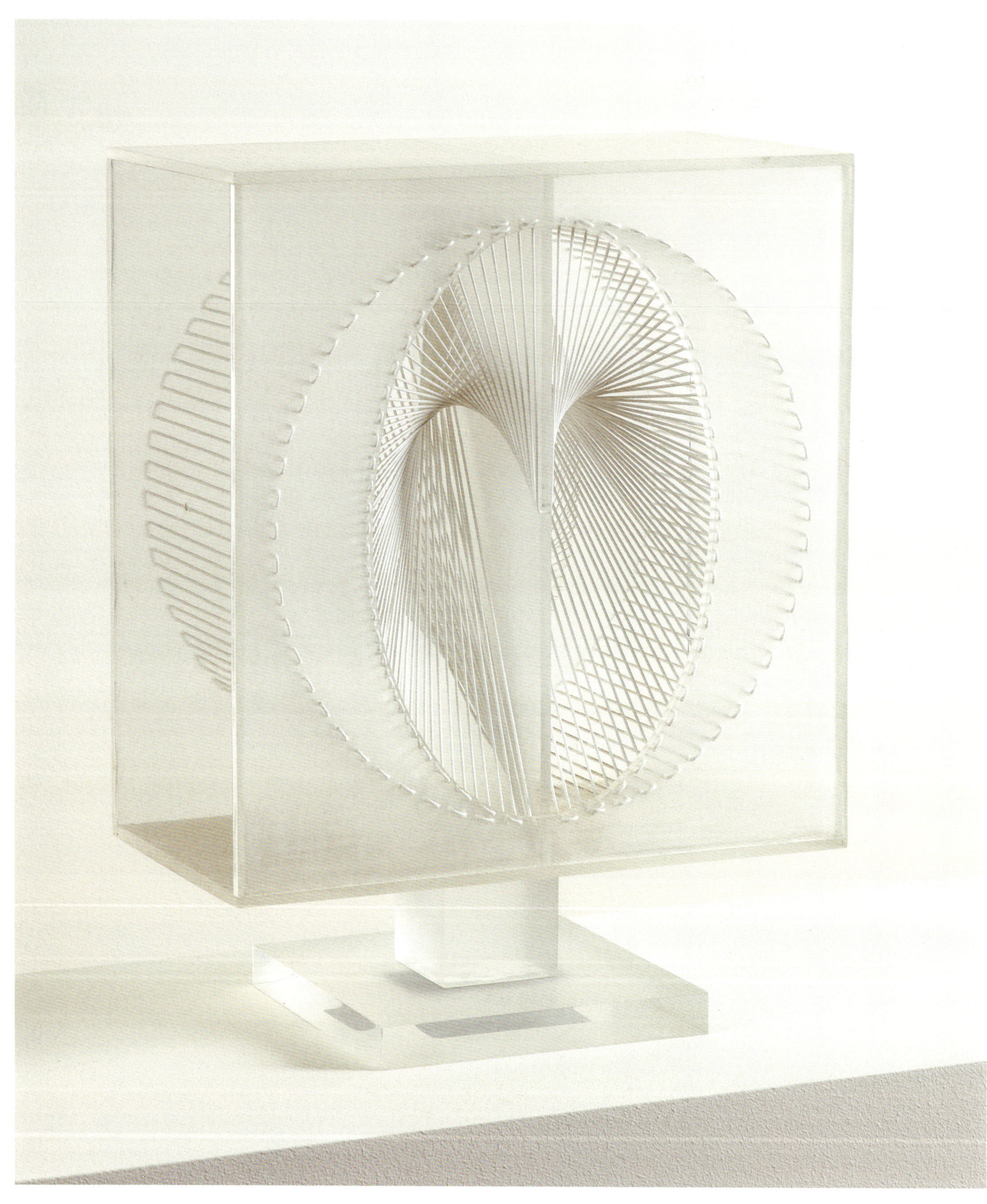

Sue Fuller, *String Composition #742*, 1986
Lucite and Teflon, 19¼ × 15 × 7⅞ in. (49 × 38 × 20 cm)

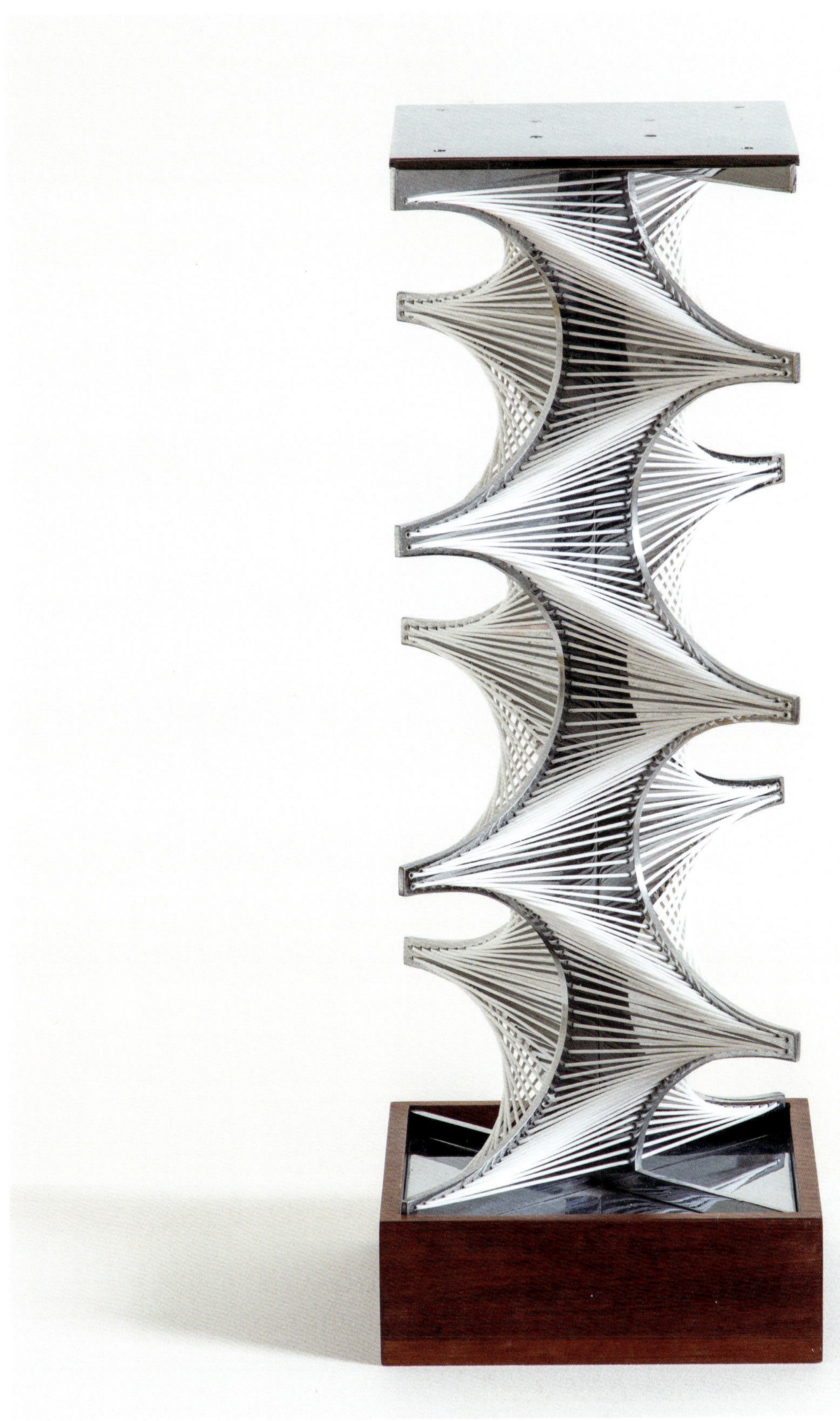

Sue Fuller, *Teflon Tower, #763*, 1990
Teflon, brass, chrome and wood, 22¼ × 8¼ × 8¼ in. (56.5 × 21 × 21 cm)

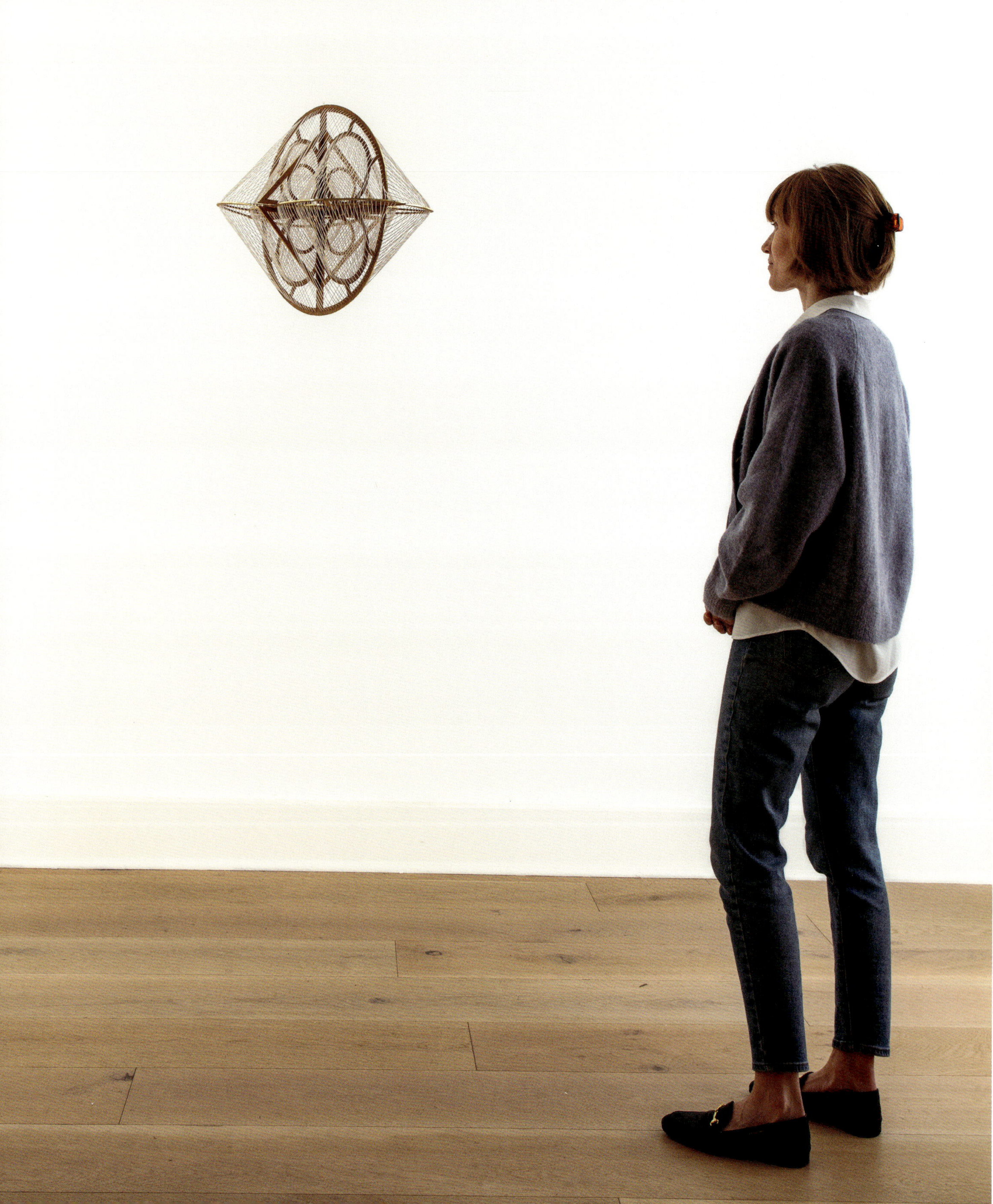

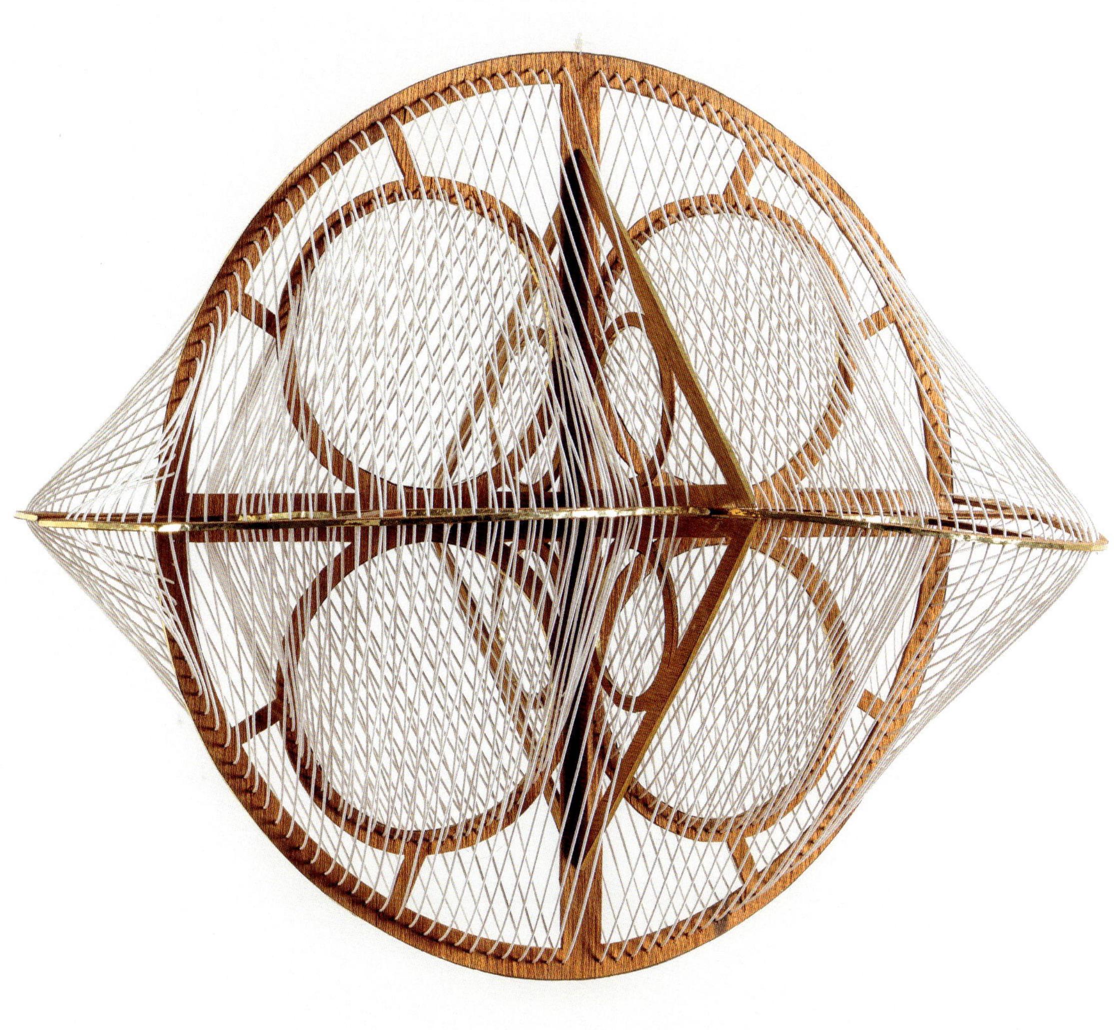

Sue Fuller, *String Composition #253*, 1984
String, wire and wood, 15 × 20 × 12 in. (38 × 51 × 30.5 cm)

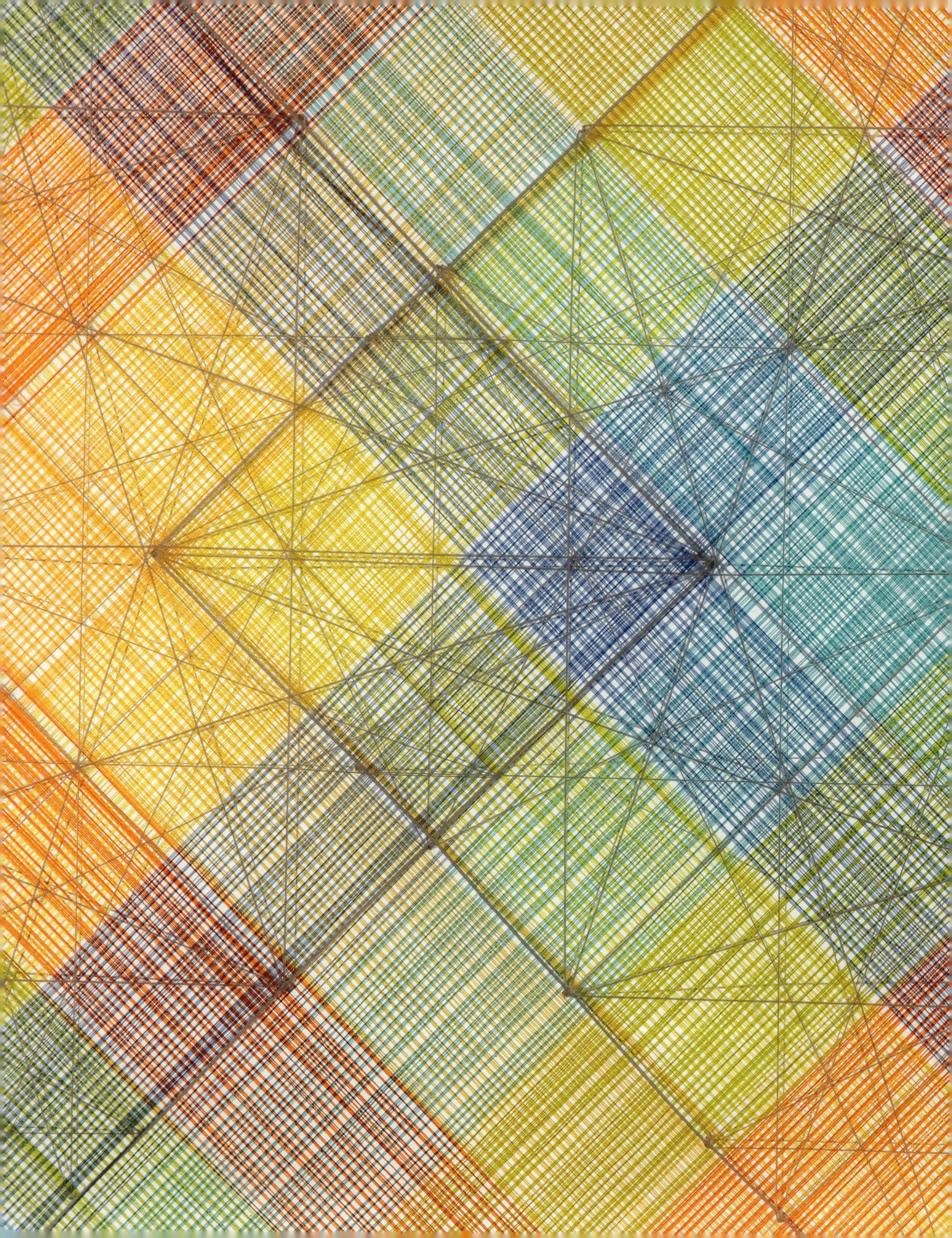

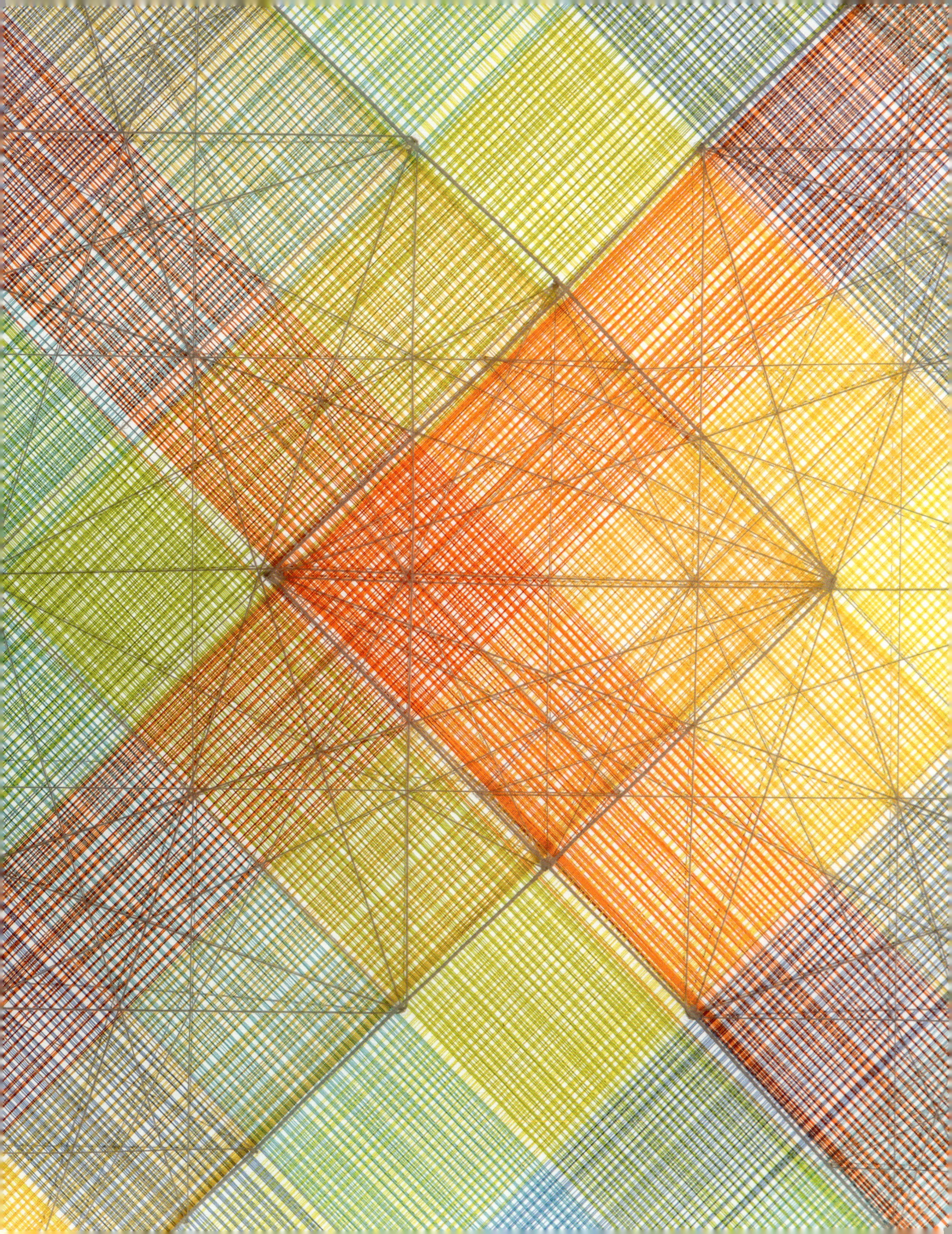

Chronology

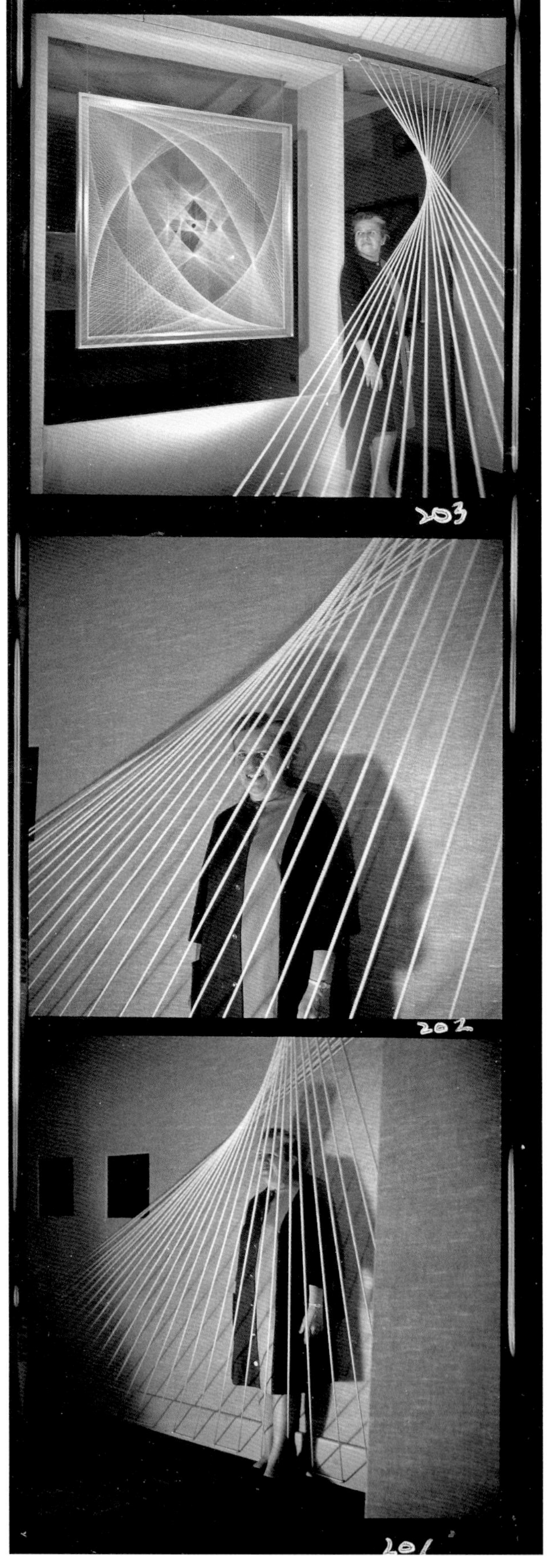

Fig.18
Installation view of *String Compositions, Plastic Embedments, Watercolors, Prints and Collages by Sue Fuller*, 28 June–28 August 1966, Storm King Art Center, New York

1914
Born Caroline Sue Fuller in Pittsburgh, Pennsylvania

1931
During the summer, studies under Ernest Thurn at the Thurn School of Art, Gloucester, Massachusetts

1932–36
Studies at the Carnegie Institute of Technology, Pittsburgh

1934
Studies under Hans Hofmann at the Thurn School of Art during the summer

1937–39
Studies at Teachers College, Columbia University, New York

1938–40
Teaches at The Principia high school, St Louis, Missouri

1939
Publishes 'Bringing Up Teacher' in *Art Education Today: An Annual Devoted to the Problems of Art Education*

1941–43
Works at the Sue Williams Display Studio making window displays for high-end New York City department stores

1943
Publishes 'Shall We Scrap the Art Teacher in Time of War' in *Design*

1943–45
Studies at Stanley William Hayter's Atelier 17 at the New School for Social Research, New York. She serves as Monitor from September 1944 to February 1945

c.1944
Meets Joseph Albers on the occasion of a workshop at the Museum of Modern Art, New York

1944
Participates in the exhibition *Hayter and Studio: New Directions in Gravure* at the Museum of Modern Art, New York, curated by James Johnson Sweeney

1944–47
Teaches in the department of education at the Museum of Modern Art

1946
Starts work on her first *String Compositions*

1947
Two solo exhibitions of prints: Village Art Center, New York, and Division of Graphic Art, Smithsonian Institution, Washington, DC

1948
Awarded the Louis Comfort Tiffany Fellowship

1949
Duo exhibition with Peter Busa at the Bertha Schaefer Gallery, New York. Fuller will continue to exhibit with the gallery until 1969

Life magazine publishes a full-page portrait of the artist and her work

1949
Awarded a Guggenheim Fellowship

1950
Publishes an article in *Magazine of Art* on the prints of Mary Cassatt

Teaches at the University of Minnesota as a guest artist in printmaking

Awarded a grant from National Institute of Arts and Letters

1951
Participates in the exhibition *Abstract Painting and Sculpture in America* at the Museum of Modern Art with *String Composition in Yellow and Grey* (1946, *String Composition #11*)

Travels to England to study glass blowing at the Stourbridge School of Arts and Crafts, near Birmingham in the West Midlands

Solo exhibition, *Collages, Prints, and String Compositions*, at the Corcoran Gallery of Art, Washington, DC

1951–52
Teaches at the University of Georgia

1952
Teaches a design workshop as part of a summer school at Teachers College, Columbia University

1953
First solo exhibition of *String Compositions* at Bertha Schaefer Gallery

1954
Travels to Japan to study calligraphy for six months (June–December)

Solo exhibition at the Nishimachi School, Tokyo

The Whitney Museum of American Art, New York, acquires *String Composition #51* (1953)

Publishes 'Twentieth Century Cat's Cradle' in *Craft Horizons*

1955
The Metropolitan Museum of Art, New York, acquires *String Composition #50* (1952–53)

Publishes 'The Art of Calligraphy: A Japanese Artist and His Tradition' in *Arts Magazine*

1956
Participates in the exhibition *Modern Art in the United States* at the Tate Gallery, London

Solo exhibition at the Marion Koogler McNay Art Institute, San Antonio, Texas

1959
A solo exhibition tours to Chatham College, Pennsylvania; Grinnell College, Iowa; and the Pioneer Museum, Stockton, California

1961
Participates in the United States Information Agency exhibition *Plastics USA*, which tours Kyiv, Moscow and Tbilisi in the Soviet Union

1962
Studies lacemaking with Marian Powys, an English-born expert in handmade lace

Participates in the exhibition *Geometric Abstraction in America* at the Whitney Museum of American Art

1965
Participates in the exhibition *The Responsive Eye* at the Museum of Modern Art with *String Composition #119* (1964)

1965–66
Teaches at the Pratt Institute, New York

1966
Solo exhibition of *String Compositions, Plastic Embedments, Watercolors, Prints and Collages* at the Storm King Art Center, New Windsor, NY

1967
Mid-career retrospective at the Marion Koogler McNay Art Institute

Solo exhibition at the Norfolk Museum of Arts and Sciences (now the Chrysler Museum), Virginia

1969
Registers a US patent for the process by which her string compositions are made

Solo exhibition, *Embedments*, at Bertha Schaefer Gallery

1974
Awarded the Alumni Merit Award by Carnegie Mellon University (formerly Carnegie Institute of Technology)

1975–77
Works with master printers Donn Steward and Janet Ruttenberg to replicate the technique used in *The Coiffure* and *In the Omnibus*, two of Mary Cassatt's colour prints from 1890–91

1977
Travels to Iraq and Iran

1978
Solo exhibition at the Port Washington Library on Long Island, NY

Participates in the exhibition *American Sculpture* at the Solomon R. Guggenheim Museum, New York

1979–80
Commissioned to produce a large chancel hanging for the Unitarian Church of All Souls in New York City. The frame measures 4 metres tall by 2.6 metres wide and uses more than 15,000 metres of fluorocarbon filament

1984
Commissioned to produce a hanging sculpture, *String Composition #W-253*, for the inauguration of the Tobin Theatre Arts Gallery at the Marion Koogler McNay Art Institute.

1986
Awarded a Lifetime Achievement Award by the Women's Caucus for Art

1990
Participates in the exhibition *A Spectrum of Innovation: Color in American Printmaking, 1890–1960* at the Amon Carter Museum, Fort Worth, Texas. The exhibition travels to the Nelson-Atkins Museum of Art, Kansas City, Missouri (1990), and the Worcester Art Museum in Massachusetts (1991)

1993
Participates in the exhibition *Atelier 17 and the New York Avant-Garde, 1940–1955* at the Pollock-Krasner House and Study Center, East Hampton, NY

2002
Solo exhibition, *Sue Fuller: Prints and Constructions, 1944 to 1965*, at the Susan Teller Gallery, New York

2004
Solo exhibition, *Sue Fuller and the New York Atelier 17*, at the Susan Teller Gallery

2006
Sue Fuller dies in Southampton, Long Island

Public collections that hold works by Sue Fuller include:

Art Institute of Chicago, Chicago, IL
Baltimore Museum of Art, Baltimore, MD
Boston Museum of Fine Arts, Boston, MA
Brooklyn Museum of Art, New York
Carnegie Museum of Art, Pittsburgh, PA
Chrysler Museum of Art, Norfolk, VA
Currier Museum of Art, Manchester, NH
Davis Museum, Wellesley College, Wellesley, MA
Detroit Institute of Arts, Detroit, MI
Flint Institute of Arts, Flint, MI
Harvard Art Museum, Cambridge, MA
High Museum of Art, Atlanta, GA
Honolulu Academy Museum of Art, Honolulu, HI
Huntington Art Collections, San Marino, CA
Indianapolis Museum of Art, Indianapolis, IN
Library of Congress, Washington, DC
McNay Art Museum, San Antonio, TX
Mead Art Museum, Amherst, MA
Memorial Art Gallery, University of Rochester, Rochester, NY
Metropolitan Museum of Art, New York
Museum of Art, Rhode Island School of Design, Providence, RI
Museum of Fine Arts, Boston, MA
Museum of Modern Art, New York
National Gallery of Art, Washington, DC
New York Public Library, New York
Oklahoma City Museum of Art, Oklahoma City, OK
Pennsylvania Academy of the Fine Arts, Philadelphia, PA
Philadelphia Museum of Art, Philadelphia, PA
Sheldon Museum of Art, Lincoln, NE
Smith College Museum of Art, Northampton, MA
Smithsonian American Art Museum, Washington, DC
St Louis Art Museum, St Louis, MO
Syracuse University Art Museum, Syracuse, NY
Tate, UK
Weisman Art Museum, Minneapolis, MN
Whitney Museum of American Art, New York
Worcester Art Museum, Worcester, MA

Published in 2022 by Ridinghouse and Luxembourg + Co.
on the occasion of the exhibition:

Sue Fuller: Into the Composition
at Luxembourg + Co., London,
10 October–9 December 2022

Luxembourg + Co.
2 Savile Row
London W1A 3PA
United Kingdom
luxembourgco.com

Ridinghouse
46 Lexington Street
London W1F 0LP
United Kingdom
ridinghouse.co.uk

Distributed in the UK, Europe and the rest of the world by
ACC Art Books
Sandy Lane, Old Martlesham
Woodbridge, Suffolk IP12 4SD
accartbooks.com

Distributed in the United States and Canada by
ARTBOOK | D.A.P.
75 Broad Street, Suite 630
New York, NY 10004
artbook.com

Cover: Detail of Sue Fuller, *Untitled*, c.1950s

Details: endpapers (details of *String Composition #338*, 1965), frontispiece, p.2 (detail of *String Composition #11*, 1946), p.4 (detail of *Test Lucite, with Color*, c.1968), pp.10–11 (detail of *String Composition #540*, 1969), p.23 (detail of *String Composition #162*, 1974), p.33 (detail of *New York, New York!*, 1949), pp.34–35 (detail of *String Composition #385*, 1971), pp.90–91 (detail of *Rectangle*, 1970)

Photography by Richard Ivey (unless otherwise stated)

British Library Cataloguing-in-Publication Data: A full catalogue record of this book is available from the British Library.

ISBN 978-1-909932-78-4

Edited by Yuval Etgar
Research and coordination: Inès Leynaud and Raphaële Sevrain
Exhibition production: Helen Kempthorne

Ridinghouse Publisher: Sophie Kullmann
Ridinghouse Senior Editor: Aimee Selby

Designed by Mark Thomson
Set in The Future
Printed in Belgium by Graphius

Supported by

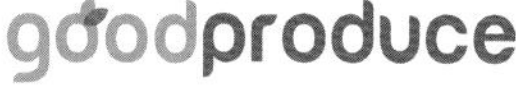

Photographic credits

p.6: Photo: Herta Sharland Forte
p.7: © 2022 The Josef and Anni Albers Foundation/Artists Rights Society (ARS), New York/DACS, London. Photo: Tolo Balaguer/Alamy Stock Photo
p.8: © DACS, 2022. Photo: Historic Collection/Alamy Stock Photo
p.8: © O Mundo de Lygia Clark-Associação Cultural, Rio de Janeiro. Photo: Marcelo Ribeiro Corrêa, Courtesy of the Lygia Clark Estate
p.9: Photo: Digital image, The Museum of Modern Art, New York/Scala, Florence
p.12: Photo: Image copyright The Metropolitan Museum of Art/Art Resource/Scala, Florence
p.16: The Work of Naum Gabo © Nina & Graham Williams. Photo: Soichi Sunami, Tate Images
p.20: Photo: Tate Images
p.24: Photo: Eileen Darby. Brooklyn Museum Archives. Department of Prints, Drawings and Photographs records: Exhibitions. 14 Painter-Printmakers [11/16/1955-01/08/1956]
p.26: Photo: Image copyright The Metropolitan Museum of Art/Art Resource/Scala, Florence
p.27: Photo: © 2022 Museum of Fine Arts, Boston
p.30: Photo: McNay Art Museum, Gift of Robert L.B. Tobin and the Friends of the McNay in honour of Margaret Batts Tobin
p.31 and p.92: Photo: Eileen Darby. © Storm King Art Center, Mountainville, New York 2022

LUXEMBOURG + CO.

Ridinghouse

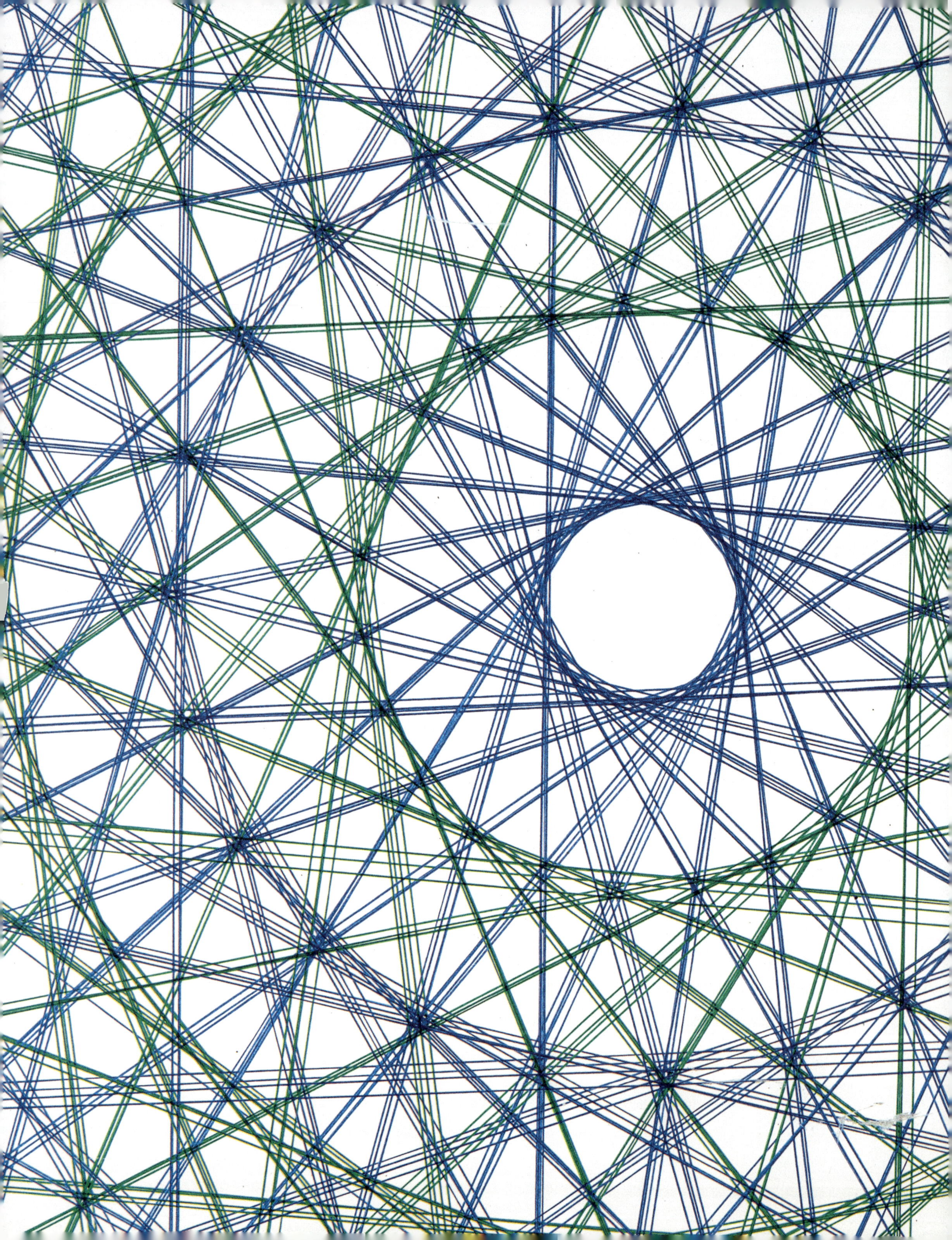